The Davidic Generation

UNDERSTANDING THIS
PRESENT MOVE OF THE SPIRIT

DAVID SWAN
(Tan Suan Chew)

The Davidic Generation

Copyright © Tan Suan Chew (David Swan)
ISBN: 983-99853-5-3
Third Printing (Revised Edition) 2002
Second Printing (Revised Edition) 1999
First Printing 1993

Unless otherwise noted, Bible quotations are
taken from the New King James Version.

Cover design and artwork by
David Swan, Kim and Christine.

The Davidic Generation

Dedicated to

**JESUS,
The Greater David**

*"... He who is holy,
He who is true,
'He who has the key of David'..."
(Rev 3:7)*

my wife, Irene

and the
precious members of
Tabernacle of David

Acknowledgements

Special thanks to Rev Susan Tang, Prophets Jim and Judy Stevens, Dr Henry Ramaya, and Prophets Vernon and Margareth Falls for contributing to the foreword. Last but not least, my heartfelt gratitude to those who have supported me in prayer.

Contents

Foreword

~Prophets Jim and Judy Stevens~

(Associate Pastor of Marion Christian Center, Ohio, USA. Ordained as prophetic ministers with C.I., Network of Prophetic Ministries under Bishop Dr Bill Hamon.)

We were honoured to minister in several of the outreach churches this apostle has begun and also to minister at the home church, Tabernacle of David, where he now pastors. Pastor David (as we call him) is a worshipper and his congregation has received impartation from his spirit of worship and have been trained to ascend into the presence of the Lord in a power and dimension unlike very few churches we have attended in any nation of the world! During that visit we looked through the rough draft of David's book, **The Davidic Generation,** and were very impressed with it. Upon receiving the "finished product" we are even more impressed and thrilled with the work the Lord has brought forth from our brother.

The spirit of revelation, working together with the experiential reality of that revelation regarding restoration and present truth, has truly been brought together in this book. We highly recommend **The Davidic Generation** as "must reading" for those with a prophetic heart and a desire to better understand the moving of God's spirit in this day and hour.

~Rev Dr Henry Ramaya~

(Senior Pastor of two large growing churches. He has planted 20 other churches and operates in the five-fold gifts ministry. Called as an apostle to the nations of the world.)

I have been associated with Rev Tan Suan Chew from the very beginning of his ministry. His lifestyle demonstrates the heart of a true shepherd - an exemplary minister and church planter.

This book is a revelation of the end-time move of God in raising a generation of holy worshippers. God cannot be entertained by today's so-called worship with dance and music by the rebellious and unholy. True worship stems from obedience and holy living; otherwise, it is strange fire. This book is a reflection of what God has already done in the life of the author.

~Rev Susan Tang~

(Pioneered numerous churches, especially in Sabah, East Malaysia. Her apostolic ministry has touched and transformed thousands of lives in the past 26 years.)

The Davidic Generation will not just usher in the final return of Jesus Christ, they will also usher Jesus back into everything! This will be a generation who will not live for the church, the ministry, the denomination, the organisation, the self, or any other glory, BUT FOR JESUS AND JESUS ALONE! They will be a generation who will live in the center and not at the circumference of Christianity.

YES! THE DAVIDIC GENERATION WILL USHER JESUS BACK INTO EVERYTHING!! All that has taken His place will be fallen...and let them fall... buildings, churches, ministries, etc...let Jesus be ushered back! Welcome, Davidic Generation! Usher Jesus back to us, our hearts have ached for Him...for too long.

~Prophets Vernon and Margareth Falls~

(Founders of Lifeline International Ministries who have a unique apostolic, prophetic, teaching and miracle healing ministry that has reached over 40 nations of the world.)

Over the years I have observed David Tan Suan Chew prayerfully, scripturally, and cautiously seek to enter into deeper revelations and dimensions of our Lord Jesus Christ. At various times, I could hear his heart reach out and cry aloud to the Lord, "Oh Lord, reveal to me more of You."

The Davidic Generation represents the many hours of prayer, fasting, worshipping, waiting, fellowshipping, and searching the Scriptures as he learnt to touch the heart of the Father.

This book will challenge you to reach out into new dimensions of God, and understand His plan and purpose for our generation.

Preface

This prophetic message and revelation on **The Davidic Generation** was birthed in my spirit during a time when God graciously granted me a powerful visitation in 1987.

Often, when I share this revelation with individuals or churches, a strong prophetic anointing comes upon me. At times, this prophetic anointing causes the atmosphere around me and the meeting place to be charged with life. Many have testified of this tangible anointing which they had sensed when this message was shared.

I felt a divine commission to "run with this revelation." It is my prayer that this book will contribute further toward our understanding of the present move of the Holy Spirit in these exciting and crucial end-times. May it help to prepare in us the right response and to flow with Him in the wonderful things that He is doing and is about to do.

This book is written from the prophetic perspective. Some of the personal testimonies shared in this book may only be applicable to the author's ministry and his church.

"For we know in part and we prophesy in part"
(1 Cor 13:9)

DAVID SWAN
(Tan Suan Chew)

Introduction

"comparing spiritual things with spiritual"
(1 Cor 2:13)

Much has been preached and written concerning The Joshua Generation. I believe this message on **The Davidic Generation** will give us additional understanding of this present end-time move of the Spirit.

There are eight major, progressive prophetic lessons in David's life which have great relevance and application for this end-time generation:

1. **David the Worshipper**
2. **David the Warrior**
3. **David Recovered All**
4. **David the Prophet**
5. **David's Multiple Anointing**
6. **David and the Ark of God**
7. **Davidic Covenant**
8. **David's Dominion**

The Davidic era is a prophetic type of this end-time generation. It precedes King Solomon's era, a type of the Millennium. David's era is characterised by much spiritual warfare whereas King Solomon's era is characterised by peace and rest.

Davidic Era	Solomon's Era
Type of the end-time generation	*Type of the Milennium*
Period of warfare and conquest	*Period of rest and peace*

God made a covenant promise with Abraham in Genesis 15:18 and stated to him the extent of the land that would be his descendants' possession. Later, in Numbers 34:1 to 15, God once again defined to Moses the territories and boundaries that should be their inheritance. These represented in type the full inheritance God intended for His people to receive:

"Then the Lord spoke to Moses, saying, 'Command the children of Israel, and say to them: When you come into the land of Canaan, this is the land that shall fall to you as an inheritance—the land of Canaan to its boundaries. Your southern border shall be...As for the western border...And this shall be your northern border...You shall mark out your eastern border from...'"

Joshua had tried his best to conquer the whole land of Canaan as commanded by God to Moses. However, when he died, there remained much land yet to be conquered.

"Now Joshua was old, advanced in years. And the Lord said to him: 'You are old, advanced in years, and **there remains very much land yet to be possessed**' *(Jos 13:1).*

*"This is **the land that yet remains**: all the territory of the Philistines and all that of the Geshurites"* (Jos 13:2).

*"Nevertheless **the children of Israel did not drive out the** Geshurites or the Maachathites..."* (Jos 13:13).

*"As for the Jebusites, the inhabitants of Jerusalem, **the children of Judah could not drive them out**; but the Jebusites dwell with the children of Judah at Jerusalem to this day"* (Jos 15:63).

*"And they **did not drive out the Canaanites** who dwelt in Gezer..."* (Jos 16:10).

*"Yet the children of Manasseh **could not drive out** the inhabitants of those cities, but the Canaanites were determined to dwell in that land"* (Jos 17:12).

*"they put the Canaanites to forced labour, but **did not utterly drive them out**"* (Jos 17:13).

"Then Joshua said to the children of Israel: 'How long will you neglect to go and possess the land which the Lord God of your fathers has given you?'" (Jos 18:3).

From the Scriptures, it is very clear that **The Joshua Generation** failed to capture the entire Promised Land. It needed another key person (representing another generation) who would be divinely endowed with special qualities to complete the conquest.

About 500 years later, God found that person (Acts 13:17-22). He was King David, a man after God's own heart. He brought the kingdom of Israel to its greatest extent and glory. This is very significant in the progressive revelation of God. King David's life is also a prophetic type of the end-time generation of Spirit-led and Spirit-activated Christians—**The Davidic Generation!**

KING DAVID

King David was Israel's greatest and most well-known king. He is one of the most colourful characters in the Bible. Sixty-six chapters of the Bible are written concerning his life, whereas there are only about fourteen chapters on the life of Abraham. David's name is mentioned in the Bible about 1,200 times! This astounding figure tells us a great deal about David.

In his lifetime, David was a shepherd, musician, composer, singer, national hero, gifted leader, writer, prophet, king, conqueror, and temple builder. King David was involved in receiving the divine revelation for the temple, providing the blueprint and preparing abundant building materials (1 Chron 22:1-5; 28:11-19; 29:1-5).

God's answer for Israel in her hour of need was to raise up David who carried out His deliverance and purpose. Hence, His answer for this end-time is to raise up The Davidic Generation that will carry out His divine end-time purpose and complete what The Joshua Generation had begun. This is a spiritual type, a prophetic representation, a thing which prefigures another, for example, "...of Adam, who was a type of Him who was to come" (Rom 5:14) and has an important lesson that is relevant to us in this present time.

The Davidic Generation is a generation of worshippers and spiritual warriors. It is a generation that will experience the restoration of all things. They will move prophetically and will be richly anointed. This generation will know the right ways of ushering the presence of God into their lives and church services. It is a generation of believers that will walk in covenant relationship with God. Many men and women of God in The Davidic Generation will have the spirit of dominion manifested in their ministry. The attributes of The Davidic Generation are further expounded in the eight chapters of this book.

King David is also a type of the Lord Jesus—the Greater David. Probably, he is the closest type of the Lord Jesus found in the Bible. The many similarities between King David and the Lord Jesus are truly amazing.

Hence, His answer for this end-time is to raise up The Davidic Generation that will carry out His divine end-time purpose and complete what The Joshua Generation had begun.

DAVID	**JESUS**
1. Born in Bethlehem *(1 Sam 17:12)*	1. Born in Bethlehem *(Luke 2:4-6)*
2. Son of Jesse *(1 Sam 16:18-19)*	2. Root of Jesse *(Isa 11:10)*
3. Name means beloved *(Ps 108:6; Zech 2:8)*	3. Beloved of the Father *(Luke 3:22)*
4. A good shepherd *(1 Sam 16:11)*	4. The Good Shepherd *(John 10:11)*
5. Misunderstood by his brothers *(1 Sam 17:28-29)*	5. Misunderstood by his brothers *(John 7:3-5)*
6. Experienced rejection *(1 Sam 30:6)*	6. Rejected by men *(Isa 53:3, John 1:11)*
7. Chosen by God *(Ps 89:3)*	7. Chosen by God *(1 Pet 2:4)*
8. Suffered humiliation *(1 Sam 21:13-15)*	8. Suffered humiliation *(Matt 27:27-31)*
9. Wilderness experience *(1 Sam 19-27)*	9. Wilderness experience *(Matt 4:1)*
10. Man of prayer *(Ps 109:4)*	10. Man of prayer *(Luke 5:16)*
11. Refused to revile in return *(2 Sam 16:5-13)*	11. He opened not His mouth *(Isa 53:7; I Pet 2:23)*

DAVID	**JESUS**
12. Gracious *(2 Sam 9)*	12. Full of grace *(John 1:14; 1 Pet 2:3)*
13. Anointed *(1 Sam 16:13; 2 Sam 23:1)*	13. The Anointed *(Isa 61:1-3; Matt 3:16)*
14. Defeated Goliath *(1 Sam 17)*	14. Defeated Satan *(Heb 2:14)*
15. After God's own heart *(Acts 13:22; 1 Sam 13:14)*	15. I delight to do Thy will *(John 4:34; 6:38)*
16. Exalted by God *(2 Sam 7:8-17)*	16. Exalted by God *(Phil 2:9)*
17. Became King over Israel at the age of 30 *(2 Sam 5:4)*	17. Began ministry at about the age of 30 *(Luke 3:23)*
18. Priest *(1 Chron 15:27)*	18. Perfect High Priest *(Heb 4:14)*
19. Prophet *(Acts 2:29-30)*	19. Supreme Prophet *(Deut 18:18-19; Acts 3:22)*
20. King of Israel *(2 Sam 5:3)*	20. King of kings *(Rev 17:14)*

Chapter 1

The Generation
That Worships Like David

1. Davidic Worship

2. The Golden Altar of Incense

3. Preparing the Atmosphere

4. Praise and Worship - Aerial Domination

5. Prophesying with Musical Instruments

6. Musical Instruments of God

7. Music and the Word

8. New Name - New Destiny and New Ministry

9. 'One Sound' Phenomenon

10. The Worship Flow

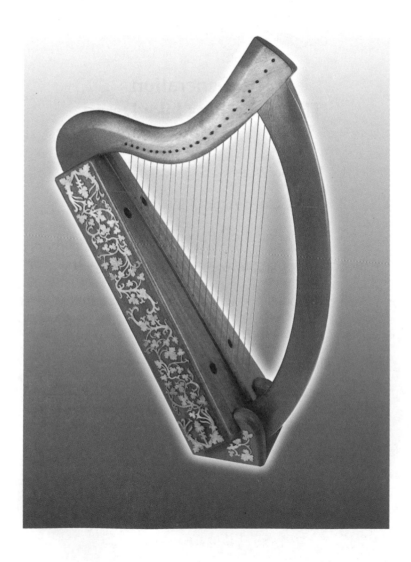

DAVIDIC WORSHIP

"He awakens me morning by morning, He awakens my ear to hear as the learned" (Isa 50:4).

"This is the generation that worships like David." I heard this distinctly in my spirit early one morning. Immediately, my spirit was alert and I was wide awake. As I pondered on these words that had been spoken into my spirit, it suddenly seemed to strongly confirm so many things. Yes! This is the generation that would worship like David. This generation would once again learn to follow the form, flow, and spontaneity of Davidic worship.

When God teaches us, He often uses the lives of certain individuals in the Bible. For example, He teaches us faith through the life of Abraham; patience through Job; prophetic ministry through Samuel, Elijah and Elisha. And when God wants to teach us worship in its most highly developed form, He does so through the life of a great worshipper - King David.

God richly bestowed upon David His Spirit, grace, gifts, insight, understanding and revelational knowledge concerning worship. Through his life and attitudes, and the Psalms (73 psalms have his authorship identified in the Bible), we can learn to worship as David did. The Psalms provide us with a great wealth of information and instructions relating to the focus, forms, expressions, and experience of worship.

God established through King David a new and

higher order of worship. This new order is different in many aspects compared to the order of worship in the Tabernacle of Moses. The death and resurrection of Jesus have changed the elements of worship found in the Tabernacle of Moses. Now, we are called to worship the Father in spirit and in truth. Davidic worship represents this kind of worship which the Father seeks.

Praise and worship is the main activity around the throne of God. It is also the activity that takes place closest to the throne. Worship is throne room ministry (Rev 4-5). The worship established by King David on Mount Zion is a type of worship in heaven. In every subsequent restoration and revival during the time of Joash, Hezekiah, Josiah, Ezra and others, the Israelites always returned to the form of worship that was established by King David. I believe Davidic worship will continue to be the form of worship in the Millennium.

The worship established by King David on Mount Zion is a type of worship in heaven.

"with rejoicing and with singing, as it was established by David...Moreover King Hezekiah and the leaders commanded the Levites to sing praise to the Lord with the words of David...following the written instruction of David king of Israel" (2 Chron 23:18; 29:30; 35:4).

THE GOLDEN ALTAR OF INCENSE

"You shall make an altar to burn incense on; you shall make it of acacia wood. A cubit shall be its length and a cubit its width—it shall be square— and two cubits shall be its height. Its horns shall be of one piece with it" (Exo 30:1-2).

The Tabernacle of Moses had three areas. The first area was called the outer court; the second, the Holy Place; and the third, the Holy of Holies. In the Holy Place were placed three articles: the Table for the showbread, the Gold Lampstand and the Altar of Incense.

The Altar of Incense, measuring about four feet high, was probably the tallest article in the Holy Place (the dimensions of the Lampstand are not given). It was placed closest to the Holy of Holies where the Ark of God was. The whole Altar was covered with gold. It had a golden crown at the top, with four golden horns at each corner. Every morning and evening, sweet incense, made from a compound of stacte, onycha, galbunam, and frankincense in equal proportion, was burned on the Altar. The Golden Altar of Incense and the sweet incense speak of the prayer, praise, worship, and intercession that ascend to God. The sweet incense is fragrant and pleasing to Him. He seeks true worshippers and takes delight in their prayers and praises.

The golden horns on the four corners of the Altar denote power. There is power in prayer, praise, worship, and intercession. An example can be found in Revelation 8:3-5, "Then another angel, having a golden censer, came and stood at the altar. And he was given much incense, that he should offer it with the prayers of all the saints upon the golden altar which was before the throne. And the smoke of the incense, with the prayers of the saints, ascended before God from the angel's hand. Then the angel took the censer, filled it with fire from the altar, and threw it to the earth. And there were noises, thunderings, lightnings, and an earthquake."

The golden horns on the four corners of the Altar denote power. There is power in prayer, praise, worship, and intercession.

The **equal proportion** of the ingredients speaks about balance and harmony. **There is beauty in a balanced life.** Prayer, praise, worship, and intercession are interrelated. For example, you cannot praise and worship well if you do not pray. When all these ingredients are present in our lives, we become like the sweet incense that is fragrant and pleasing to God.

The height of the Golden Altar of Incense speaks of the 'high' ministry at this altar. Dr Larry Lea says, "The call to prayer is the highest calling." The Holy Spirit is involved in intercession for us. He intervenes on our behalf. "Likewise the Spirit also helps in our weaknesses. For we do not know what we should pray for as we ought, but the Spirit Himself makes intercession for us with groanings which cannot be uttered" (Rom 8:26). Jesus is also involved with the ministry of intercession today. "It is Christ who died, and furthermore is also risen, who is even at the right hand of God, who also makes intercession for us" (Rom 8:34).

The Altar of Incense was placed closest to the Holy of Holies, directly facing the Ark of God. When the high priest entered the Holy of Holies during the Day of Atonement, he took with him in his hands much sweet incense and a censer full of burning coals from the altar.

*"Then he shall take a censer **full** of burning coals of fire from the altar before the Lord, with his hands **full** of sweet incense beaten fine, and bring it inside the veil" (Lev 16:12).*

This shows us that the way for us to move from the Holy Place into the realm of the Holy of Holies (besides being cleansed and sanctified by blood) is through much prayer, praise, worship, and intercession. **Those whose lives are full of it will be able to move deeper into the presence of God.**

In Hebrews 9:2-4, the Altar of Incense is mentioned in the Holy of Holies, together with the Ark of God. I do not believe there is an error here. I believe the inclusion of the Altar of Incense in the Holy of Holies is deliberate. The author of the book of Hebrews, by revelation, realised that the high priest in the Old Testament could only enter in once a year, with the blood of the animal sacrifice, and the censer and incense. However, in the New Testament, we read that Jesus shed His blood once and for all, so that we may now enter into the Holiest of all—but not without the censer that is **full** of burning coals and sweet incense, that is, much prayer, praise, worship, and intercession.

Upon reading the book of Psalm, you will realise that prayer, praise, worship, and intercession were integral parts of David's life. The book of Psalm is a compilation of hymns, prayers, and prophecies. Many of the psalms begin as prayer and end with prophecies and promises from God. They are poetry, comprising spiritual insight and deepest feeling. The entire spectrum of human emotion is expressed in them. Spontaneity and prophetic inspiration are also distinctive features in David's psalms and worship.

Prophetic worship is one of the keys to the manifestation of God's presence.

Prophetic worship is one of the keys to the manifestation of God's presence. Often, during such times when the presence of God is strong, revelations are received. In this Davidic Generation, the sweet incense of prayer, praise, worship and intercession is rising more and more unto God, ascending to His throne. Through these spiritual activities, this Davidic Generation will be brought to a greater intimacy with God. And, as they behold Him in His glory, they are being transformed into His glorious image by the Spirit of the Lord (2 Cor 3:18).

"according to the custom of the priesthood, his lot fell to burn incense when he went into the temple of the Lord. And the whole multitude of the people was praying outside at the hour of incense. Then an angel of the Lord appeared to him, standing on the right side of the altar of incense" (Luke 1:9-11).

PREPARING THE ATMOSPHERE

"The earth was without form, and void; and darkness was on the face of the deep. And the Spirit of God was hovering over the face of the waters. Then God said..." (Gen 1:2-3).

Here is an important lesson for us to take note of. The moving of God's Spirit precedes the preaching of His Word. Ministers of the Word should learn to 'read the atmosphere'. If the atmosphere is not conducive for the Word to be preached, they must change the atmosphere to get optimum results.

The spiritual atmosphere can be changed by getting the congregation to pray in unison for a while, to worship longer or to humble themselves until the anointing descends. One of the most effective means to do this is to get them to pray and sing in tongues. **Sustained and spontaneous singing in the Spirit enables their spirits to rise easily.**

However, following the leading of the Holy Spirit is the most important key to liberate a meeting.

"It is the Spirit who gives life, the flesh profits nothing. The words that I speak to you are spirit, and they are life" (John 6:63).

"not of the letter but of the Spirit; for the letter kills, but the Spirit gives life" (2 Cor 3:6).

PRAISE AND WORSHIP - AERIAL DOMINATION

In the 1991 Gulf War, during "The Desert Storm" operation, the coalition forces enjoyed complete aerial domination. The Iraqi army, which was deprived of air cover and support became very vulnerable to the daily air strikes. Subsequently, when the ground war began, it was almost like a walk-over. The praise and worship of the church service can be likened to aerial warfare. Spiritual opposition and resistance are broken by intensive prayer, fervent praise and deep worship. When the atmosphere is completely liberated, the ministry of God's Word becomes easy and it ministers to the congregation. Intensive, fervent praise and worship are powerful in breaking down spiritual opposition and resistance. The breakthrough in praise and worship is the stepping stone to other spiritual breakthroughs.

"Now when they began to sing and to praise, the Lord set ambushes against the people of Ammon, Moab, and Mount Seir, who had come against Judah; and they were defeated" (2 Chron 20:22).

PROPHESYING WITH MUSICAL INSTRUMENTS

*"Moreover David and the captains of the army separated for the service some...who should **prophesy** with harps, stringed instruments, and cymbals...under the direction of Asaph, who **prophesied** according to the order of the king...who **prophesied** with a harp to give thanks and to praise the Lord" (1 Chron 25:1-3).*

One may prophesy through words, songs, mime, dance, and even through musical instruments. To prophesy with the musical instruments, the spirit of the musicians must be keenly attuned to the Holy Spirit. Prophetic music is produced when the musician is able to interpret and express what the Holy Spirit is emphasising. As the Holy Spirit moves, what is perceived in the spirit realm is translated into edifying sounds that minister and inspire. The ability to play instruments by 'ear' is helpful in this respect. New tunes and spontaneous music are often created as a result. Synchronizing with the flow of the Holy Spirit is important when prophesying with musical instruments. Prophetic music and sounds enhance the anointing. They also help to spread and sustain the anointing during a service.

Prophetic music is produced when the musician is able to interpret and express what the Holy Spirit is emphasising.

11

The musicians in my church are given the liberty and encouragement to prophesy with their instruments. It has been impressed upon them that the Holy Spirit is the actual conductor of the prophetic music team. Therefore, they should learn to follow His leading and promptings. For example, when the anointing rests upon the pianist, he or she may play spontaneously. Likewise, the other musicians may take turns to prophesy with their instruments individually or collectively, as the Holy Spirit gives them inspiration. When they are playing under the Holy Spirit's inspiration and anointing, the music produced is distinctly different. It has a greater power of edification, depth, and fluidity.

This kind of prophetic music draws us into a greater consciousness of His presence. See, for example, the case of Elisha and the minstrel, "'But now bring me a musician.' And it happened, when the musician played, that the hand of the Lord came upon him. And he said, 'Thus says the Lord...'" (2 Kgs 3:15-16).

The following verses give us another example of the effects and power of prophetic anointing and music:

"And it will happen, when you have come there to the city, that you will meet a group of prophets coming from the high place with a stringed instrument, a tambourine, a flute, and a harp before them; and they will be prophesying. Then the Spirit of the Lord will come upon you, and you will prophesy with them and be turned into another man" *(1 Sam 10:5-6).*

MUSICAL INSTRUMENTS OF GOD

"the musical instruments of God" (1 Chron 16:42).

"four thousand praised the Lord with musical instruments, 'which I made,' said David, 'for giving praise'" (1 Chron 23:5).

"And the priests attended to their services; the Levites also with instruments of the music of the Lord, which King David had made to praise the Lord..." (2 Chron 7:6).

When the anointing is upon yielded musicians, the instruments become the extension and expression of the musicians. While the anointing upon a preacher is released mainly through his words, the anointing upon musicians is released mainly through their music.

David was an anointed and skillful musician. The Scriptures record the effect of David's anointed music upon the troubled and tormented King Saul. "David would take a harp and play it with his hand. Then Saul would become refreshed and well, and the distressing spirit would depart from him" (1 Sam 16:23).

Note that three things happened:
1. Saul became **refreshed.**
2. He **recovered.**
3. He was **released** - the distressing spirit departed from him.

In the Old Testament, certain musical instruments

were also used to invoke the help of God during times of war. Seven ram horns were used during the overthrow of Jericho. "So the people shouted when the priests blew the trumpets. And it happened when the people heard the sound of the trumpet, and the people shouted with a great shout, that the wall fell down flat. Then the people went up into the city, every man straight before him, and they took the city" (Jos 6:20). Trumpets were used in the battle between Judah and Israel: "And when Judah looked around, to their surprise the battle line was at both front and rear; and they cried out to the Lord, and the priests sounded the trumpets" (2 Chron 13:14).

In the hands of anointed musicians, the musical instruments become potent spiritual weapons of war. May churches realise the importance of investing in the music department, in musicians and musical instruments.

"Every stroke the Lord lays on them with His punishing rod will be to the music of tambourines and harps, as He fights them in battle with the blows of His arm" (Isa 30:32 NIV).

MUSIC AND THE WORD

It was during King David's reign that the combination of music and the Word took on a new significance. King David took great delight in music. Being an accomplished musician himself, he encouraged and promoted the use of musical instruments in worship. He organised an orchestra and formed a choir. The chief musician was probably commissioned by King

David to add music to some of the lyrics and psalms that he wrote. The Psalms are the Word of God sung with musical accompaniment. The Word is not only read, preached or chanted; it has melody added to it. Music gives the Word wider and more creative expression. Scriptures that are set to a tune are easier to remember.

Singing together helps to unify the worshippers and enables the Word to be declared in unison. When the Word is combined with music and the Spirit, and expressed through a congregation of true worshippers, tremendous power, life and anointing are released.

It was during King David's reign that the combination of music and the Word took on a new significance.

NEW NAME - NEW DESTINY AND NEW MINISTRY

"You shall be called by a new name, which the mouth of the Lord will name" (Isa 62:2).

"No longer shall your name be called Abram, but your name shall be Abraham; for I have made you a father of many nations" (Gen 17:5).

"And God said to him, 'Your name is Jacob; your name shall not be called Jacob anymore, but Israel shall be your name'" (Gen 35:10).

"He said, 'You are Simon the son of Jonah. You shall be called Cephas'" (John 1:42).

The church I pioneered in late 1976 was called Siloam Assembly of God. I chose this name for the church because we had a significant number of visually handicapped students when the church first began.

It was to the pool of Siloam that Jesus sent the blind man to wash. The blind man obeyed and came back seeing (John 9:7).

Siloam also means "sent." This had been the main thrust of our church ministry where we sent out workers, members, and finances for the next ten years. The Lord raised up many full-time workers from our congregation. Eight other churches were planted through Siloam Assembly of God. Our aim was to have twelve outreaches within twelve years but we were held back partly by financial constraints.

1987 was a special spiritual milestone in my walk with the Lord. It was a year filled with divine visitations and outpourings of the Holy Spirit both upon my life and upon the church members.

There were also periods of intensive prayer and seeking the Lord. It was during one such period of seeking and prayer that the Holy Spirit placed within me the desire to change the church's name. It was as if the destiny of the church was to be changed together with the change in name. In fact, one morning, a missionary who was staying with my family at the time enquired if I was considering a change in the church's name! The Lord gave me another confirmation through this missionary.

During such periods of seeking the Lord, it was my habit to sleep downstairs in the living room so as not to disturb the rest of the family when I was called to prayer at odd hours. On one such night, I was awakened by the strong presence of God in the living room. Then I heard an audible voice speaking into my right ear, "Tabernacle of David! Tabernacle of David!"

It was a voice of great clarity and unusual authority. When He spoke, the voice penetrated and reverberated within my whole being. For a moment, I dared not move. I felt the awesome presence of God. It was like a host of angels were in the room too. The whole atmosphere was charged with life. Still lying down, I turned my head slowly to see who had spoken. But I did not see anyone. Then I looked at the clock and noticed it was about 3.30 in the morning. I was very excited.

I knew that the Lord had given me the new name for the church. After a while, I made my way upstairs to share the experience with my wife. Upon entering the bedroom, I was surprised to see her awake and sitting up in bed. Unknown to me, Irene also had a visitation at the same time that I had mine. She narrates her experience:

"I was awakened by a strong gust of wind that blew into the room. The curtains flew up touching the ceiling. I sat up in bed. I was very aware that together with the wind a presence had swept into the room. The awesome, yet peaceful presence was beyond description. It can only be experienced when one enters into the holy presence of God. In fact, the room seemed to have lit up with a kind of brightness. Simultaneously, this Scripture, 'Lift up your heads, O you gates! And be lifted up, you everlasting doors! And the King of Glory shall come in,' kept arising in my spirit. Immediately, my spirit rose within me. I was enjoying His presence when my husband walked into the bedroom. He said, 'Tabernacle of David' and I understood."

When the Lord gave me this name for the church, I knew that it held the key to the ministry and destiny of the church. The Bible speaks of God restoring the Tabernacle of David in the last days (Acts 15:16). I believe that this also refers to the restoration of Davidic worship.

Later, when I shared the whole experience and its significance with my congregation, they unanimously agreed to change the church's name to Tabernacle of David. Since then, we have begun to see the Lord's hand guiding and anointing us in a greater measure. He is leading us to raise up a prophetic company of people who will worship as David did. Many visitors and guest speakers have testified to being touched by the strong presence of God in our services. Often, they say they have seldom experienced such depth of worship and strong presence of God.

The Lord is continuing to teach and lead us by His

Spirit in this direction, developing and maturing us in the dimension of prophetic worship. It is a worship that flows beautifully and is inspired by the Holy Spirit.

Coincidentally, while writing this book, I heard that Dr Paul Yonggi Cho (apostle and pastor of the largest church in the history of Christendom) has changed his name to David Yonggi Cho. Though the name David was given to him by the Lord many years ago, (it is interesting to note that) the Lord reminded him of it again, on Resurrection Sunday in 1992. So, it was just recently that he changed his name to David.

'ONE SOUND' PHENOMENON

"indeed it came to pass, when the trumpeters and singers were as one, to make **one sound** *to be heard in praising and thanking the Lord, and when they lifted up their voice with the trumpets and cymbals and instruments of music, and praised the Lord...the house of the Lord, was filled with a cloud, so that the priests could not continue ministering because of the cloud; for the glory of the Lord filled the house of God" (2 Chron 5:13-14).*

This phenomenon took place during the church's 8th anniversary service in 1984. I remember it well. One of our church deacons, Jason, was the worship leader for that special occasion.

On that Sunday, the presence of God was made manifest in a glorious manner. At one point in the service, we went into high praise. The musicians' guitars, piano and drums were all playing. Suddenly, the voices of the worshippers and sound of the music seemed to 'expand'. We hit a kind of resonance.

I was praising God aloud, almost shouting. Suddenly, I could not hear my own voice. The sound of all the musical instruments became indistinguishable, merged into one growing sound. It was like absolute harmony. The 'one sound' was doubly amplified and seemed to 'jump' or 'leap up', rapidly building up to a crescendo. I was amazed. The sound was like one expanding high soprano "ahh ... ah ... Ah ... AHH ... AHHHH ..."

It dawned upon me that something very unusual was taking place. The pianist, Joshua, was so taken aback that he stopped playing - to listen. It was definitely not a sound caused by the P.A. system feedback. It was unique. Some members were also aware of the strange happening. Others were so engrossed worshipping that they were not fully aware of the phenomenon being witnessed. Many were weeping in His presence.

It was the only time such an event happened during a church service. Since then, we have not experienced a recurrence of this phenomenon. I have heard it been said that it is very difficult, even for professional musicians, to harmonise into 'one sound' as described in the Bible in 2 Chronicles 5:13 to 14. This could only have been wrought by God. On that auspicious 8th anniversary service, God's Spirit must have moved upon us very graciously. In

Scriptures, the numeral '8' speaks of a new beginning. It is also the number for our Lord Jesus Christ. Incidentally, the address of our church then was, 8 Jalan Swee Guat, Kuala Lumpur!

The Lord has constantly encouraged us with many signs and wonders throughout the years. The 'one sound' phenomenon was one of them. Some members and I greatly cherish such wonderful encouragement through these signs and wonders we have received from the Lord. All praise and glory to His wonderful name!

"I will remember the works of the Lord; surely I will remember your wonders of old. I will also meditate on all Your work, and talk of Your deeds" (Ps 77:11-12).

THE WORSHIP FLOW

If we want the worship in a service to flow prophetically, there are some practical instructions for pastors and worship leaders to take note of:

1. Appoint worship leaders who are worshippers themselves.

2. Appoint worship leaders who are sensitive to the Holy Spirit. Preferably, those who have the prophetic anointing.

3. Appoint worship leaders who are able to pitch and sing correctly.

4. Use songs or choruses which are ringing in your heart and which minister to you.

5. Be open to the Holy Spirit's leading and be prepared for a change of direction.

6. Use songs that link up well, for example, songs that have the same key, tempo, and theme.

7. A short pre-service prayer time involving the congregation helps prepare their hearts and the atmosphere for the service.

8. Have musicians who can also play by ear (hearing).

9. Talking should be kept to a minimum (let the preacher do the talking).

10. Try to minimise physical distractions and unnecessary movements in the meeting place.

11. Work out a simple set of hand signals in order to communicate with the musicians and the overhead projector operator.

12. Do not peak too often in praise and worship, unless it is natural to do so.

13. If the presence of God is already manifest at the beginning of the service, one may move straight into worship without going through the praise routine.

14. Do not attempt to teach more than one new song in a service.

15. A catalogued, low filing cabinet can be used for fast retrieval of the O.H.P. transparencies, should there be a need to sing a different song.

16. Generally, one should not use the tambourine for slower songs and during times of worship.

17. Invest in musical instruments and a good P.A. system.

When God wanted to choose a king, He chose a worshipper.

"You shall love the Lord your God with all your heart, with all your soul, with all your strength, and with all your mind..." (Luke 10:27).

TESTIMONIES – International Intercessors and Worshippers Congress (2 to 3 December 1998)

It was just awesome. What a privilege and honour as an intercessor to lift Malaysia before Jesus in the midst of the people of God with an amazing overflow of a corporate anointing. Throughout the two days I could only cry out, "Oh God! Oh God! Oh God!" It was a cry of my spirit as we were just immersed in worship of the Father, Son and Holy Spirit.

On the last night, I could hear the voice of God thundering and asking the heavenly host, "Should I look upon this nation?" Then I heard the heavenly host answering God saying, "Holy are You Most awesome God. Yes, look upon this nation for the censer overflows with their sacrifices of praise and worship with intercession."

Hallelujah! Praise the Lord! There is only one way to describe the two days: A divine appointment for

Malaysia with the sovereign God, our Lord Jesus Christ. You can only leave with the assurance of breakthrough in all the land. Glory be to God! Amen and amen!

NITIA KALUNAHARAN (Rawang, Malaysia)

◆ ◆ ◆ ◆ ◆ ◆ ◆ ◆

At the closing stage of the Congress at around 10.00 to 10.30 pm when many of the tambourine dancers and the young man with the crown walked in with slow music, I saw a bright light shining down and I saw angels coming down slowly to the center of the stadium. I only saw the lower part of the angels as in a bowing down position. It is 75% shining gold and 25% white linen. Then I saw King Jesus with His crown full of glory (His head to toe full of glow) strode majestically from the center podium to the back. All the angels filled the floor and were bowing down towards the King. When the King turned and faced my direction, I could not see how He looks like but only the glowing from His crown to His feet and suddenly my heart trembled and my lung filled with joy (a feeling of plenty of air waiting to erupt). Immediately, I erupted with a loud shout.

BERNARD LIM KONG HEAN (Petaling Jaya, Malaysia)

◆ ◆ ◆ ◆ ◆ ◆ ◆ ◆

I thoroughly enjoyed myself in the wonderful worship atmosphere. The atmosphere was electric! Many times I could only kneel and bow in worship. I was not able to pray for the participants' safe journey home on the final night because the atmosphere was too awesome for me to pray. Many were moved to tears including a number of leaders from my church. (Daniel Ho was one of the Congress speakers).

REV DANIEL K C HO (Damansara Utama, Malaysia)

◆◆◆◆◆◆◆◆

Our church members who attended the Congress testified to heaven-like worship experiences. Their experiences confirmed what God has been doing in our local worships but until the Congress, many were apprehensive as to whether they are of God. Now they are bolder to step into the Glory realm worship. The Sunday worship back home at our local church (immediately after the Congress) lasted for 4 hours and some said that it's not enough, as there was so much joy and pleasure in God's Presence. God is waking up some at odd hours to hear songs like 'Prepare Ye The Way' and also His rhemas. There's a revival of God's spoken/prophetic words in our church. Prostrating is becoming common as we approach the Holy of Holies.

PASTOR GRACE DAN (Kuantan, Malaysia)

◆◆◆◆◆◆◆◆

I am an Australian High school teacher teaching computer studies. Some of my family members live in Singapore. In a recent visit to my brother's church Tabernacle of Fire, the pastor of the church told me about the Congress. I therefore registered completely by faith with no idea what I was in for!! I participated in the International Intercessors Congress in December 2 and 3 as a flag bearer. It was the most awesome experience of my life!!! I returned home to Australia unable to put the experience behind me. It has truly gripped my heart. I have been praying for a release to worship God this way for so long. I feel privileged to have been one of the flag bearers and to have interceded for the nations with so many believers.

MRS SHIRLEY FENNELL (Australia)

◆◆◆◆◆◆◆◆

Last December '98, during the Worshippers and Intercessors Congress in Shah Alam Indoor Stadium, I was so blessed as the whole stadium was caught up in worship. I saw, in an open vision, clouds pouring in on the north side of the stadium. It seemed to be announcing the entrance of the Lord as we worshipped. That same night, as Rev David Swan led us in worship with the glory sound, I saw the Lord seated on the throne and around the foot of the throne were globes of gold. These globes burst into flames and angels came and took them in their hands. The fires became like bow and arrows in their hands. They shot the arrows and I saw myself lifted above the stadium [in the vision, the roof was missing]. They shot it all around from the stadium and in the distance I saw flashes of light as if the places were bombed. I saw other angels flying pass me and the fire of arrows were exactly like rocket bombs in their hands. The next morning, again during the worship time, I saw in a vision, angels going up and down a stairway that goes right into heaven. In the distance, I saw the bright outline of one sitting on a throne. Those angels that were ascending the stairway were carrying trays of golden globes to Him who is seated! During one of the sessions, all the tambourine dancers were prostrated before the Lord. In a flash, I saw a very big angel covered in colorful garment prostrating too.

PASTOR JEREMIAH GAN (Malaysia)

Then another angel, having a golden censer, came and
stood at the altar. And he was given much incense, that
he should offer it with the prayers of all the saints upon
the golden altar which was before the throne. And the
smoke of the incense, with the prayers of the saints,
ascended before God from the angel's hand.

(Rev 8:3-4)

Chapter 2

The Warrior Generation

1. David the Warrior

2. Spirit of David

3. Spirit of the Warriors

4. A Time to Roar

5. Cataclysmic Confrontation

6. Spiritual Warfare and Coverings

7. Jehovah Nissi

8. Weapons of Warfare

DAVID THE WARRIOR

*"Look, I have seen a son of Jesse the Bethlehemite
...**a mighty man of valor, a man of war**..."*
(1 Sam 16:18).

There was a time during the reign of King Saul when
the Philistines' armies and the men of Israel were
arrayed for battle, impasse for forty days, across a
valley. The champion of the Philistines was the giant
Goliath. He went forward and cried out to the armies
of Israel, "Why have you come out to line up for
battle? Am I not a Philistine, and you the servants of
Saul? Choose a man for yourselves, and let him
come down to me. If he is able to fight with me and
kill me, then we will be your servants. But if I prevail
against him and kill him, then you shall be our
servants and serve us. I defy the armies of Israel this
day; give me a man, that we may fight together."

When Saul and all Israel heard these words of the
Philistine, they were dismayed and greatly afraid.
And the Philistine drew near and presented himself
forty days, morning and evening. Nobody in Israel's
camp dared go forward to meet the challenge. None
dared to fight the formidable and towering Goliath.

It happened that a young Israelite lad, David, was
asked by his father to deliver food to his brothers at
the battle front. While he was there, he heard about
Goliath's taunt and challenge. To the surprise of the
men of Israel, David volunteered to fight Goliath. He
seemed to be the most unlikely candidate to fight the
giant. In fact, his brothers were chagrined and
despised him for having the audacity to think he

31

could fight Goliath. "Just who does he think he is? He's never been to war, he's untrained in battle, and he's not even old enough to be enlisted in the army", they must have thought contemptuously to themselves. Unknown and unseen by his brothers or others, David was trained by the Lord Himself while he was in the fields tending the sheep. "But God has chosen the foolish things of the world to put to shame the wise, and God has chosen the weak things of the world to put to shame the things which are mighty; and the base things of the world and the things which are despised God has chosen, and the things which are not, to bring to nothing the things that are, that no flesh should glory in His presence" (1 Cor 1:27-29).

God has an answer to the spiritual challenges and threats of the enemy in this end-time: The Davidic Generation!

God's answer to Goliath's challenge was David! David was a warrior king. His courageous feats of slaying the lion, bear, and Goliath have continued to inspire multitudes of believers throughout the generations. His other heroic exploits, victories, and conquests endeared him to all of Israel.

Likewise, God has an answer to the spiritual challenges and threats of the enemy in this end-time:

The Davidic Generation! A Warrior Generation. A generation of Spirit-filled believers who will be like David, the fearless warrior of the Lord. When these warriors of the Lord arise all over the land, many will be shocked. Shocked, because many seemingly contemptible people will have such power and authority and do great exploits just like David. These are men and women who are not trained by man but by the Almighty Himself!

In the past, there were a few known mighty men and women of God living in different times and eras. However, in this Davidic Generation and the present move of the Spirit, thousands upon thousands of mighty men and women of God are arising all over the world, simultaneously! Unknown to the public or the mass media, multitudes of them are having spiritual breakthroughs and doing great exploits for God. Mighty signs and wonders are being wrought through them and more and more of these spiritual warriors are emerging. The Warrior Generation is here! A generation of giant slayers, a generation that does great exploits!

"For by thee I have run through a troop; and by my God have I leaped over a wall" (Ps 18:29 KJV).

"I can do all things through Christ who strengthens me" (Phil 4:13).

The Warrior Generation is here! A generation of giant slayers, a generation that does great exploits!

SPIRIT OF DAVID

"And everyone who was in distress, everyone who was in debt, and everyone who was discontented gathered to him. So he became captain over them. And there were about four hundred men with him" (1 Sam 22:2).

When David was at the cave of Adullam, a motley bunch of renegades and malcontents came to join him. From the descriptions in 1 Samuel 22:2, these men seem to be nothing but a bunch of failures. However, David became their leader, and as these men associated with him, they were marvelously changed. David's excellent spirit and the anointing that was upon him soon influenced and transformed these 'below-average materials' into a feared and powerful contingent of fighting men. They caught the spirit that was in David. From ordinary men, they became brave warriors and men of valour.

These men were changed through associating with the Lord's anointed. Likewise, we will be changed as we associate with the Lord, the Mighty Warrior, and His anointed servants. When we 'catch' the same spirit they have, we will also be inspired to do great exploits for God. Love begets love, faith begets faith and a mighty man of God begets mighty men of God.

SPIRIT OF THE WARRIORS

*"The Lord shall go forth like a mighty man; He shall stir up His zeal like **a man of war**. He shall cry*

*out, yes, shout aloud; He shall prevail against His
enemies" (Isa 42:13).*

As David was a mighty warrior, the Davidic
Generation will also be a generation of spiritual
warriors. The Lord is stirring up and inspiring a new
vigour, boldness and holy aggression in the spirit of
believers. God did not give us a spirit of cringing fear.
This kind of fear has a crippling and paralysing effect
on lives. It is an enemy. A dancer who is tense with
fear, loses fluidity and gracefulness in movement.
The singer who has stage fright will lose vocal
quality. Fear affects us in a negative way in many
aspects of life. Very often, it hinders us from doing or
becoming our best.

**The Lord is stirring up
and inspiring a new vigour,
boldness and holy aggression
in the spirit of believers.**

In the book of Hebrews, we read that it is people of
boldness and faith who have accomplished much as
well as achieved some of the greatest feats. Through
such bold faith they have subdued kingdoms, worked
righteousness, obtained promises, stopped the
mouths of lions, quenched the violence of fire,
escaped the edge of the sword, were made strong
out of weakness, became valiant in battle, and turned
to flight the armies of the aliens.

The services of churches, in which the worshipping warriors have already risen, are different. The praise and worship of the congregation is triumphant and energetic. And there is great fervency in their prayer and intercession.

More believers are becoming warriors in the spirit. They have a new understanding of their authority in Jesus Christ. They will arise and exert this spiritual authority in Jesus' name. **Anointed and empowered by the Holy Spirit, they will exercise their ability to bless, prophesy, command and decree in the Spirit.**

"Thou shalt also decree a thing, and it shall be established unto thee..." (Job 22:28 KJV).

I believe imprecatory prayers, like those found in the Psalms, will be used more often and with greater results, so that those who do evil may be judged and caused to fear God. A good example in the New Testament can be found in Acts 13:8-12, the account of Paul and Elymas, the sorcerer.

"To execute on them the written judgment—this honor have all His saints" (Ps 149:9).

"So great fear came upon all the church and upon all who heard these things" (Acts 5:11).

Worshippers will move from praise to warfare praise, from worship to prophetic worship. They will enter into the 'Holy of Holies' in worship and come out with fresh power to subdue the forces of darkness.

A TIME TO ROAR

"He will roar like a lion. When He roars, then His sons shall come trembling from the west" *(Hos 11:10).*

Jesus is not only the Lamb of God, but also the mighty Lion of Judah. The Lion of Judah has begun to roar against the spiritual forces of darkness. This mighty roar is increasing in volume and power through the great army of spiritual warriors. The roar of praise, worship, and warfare is rising and intensifying throughout the world. It is ascending into the heavenlies. It is beginning to destroy satanic strongholds and to cast down evil principalities. The prowess of the Lion of Judah is being revealed through His saints.

This paean and crescendo of praise, worship, intercession, and warfare is unstoppable! Praise warriors, worshipping warriors and prayer warriors are being raised by the Spirit of God in multitudes all over the world. The build-up of this victorious army will continue until a mighty shaking takes place in the heavenlies. The forces of darkness will be defeated and disarmed. There will be an open heaven (for a season). Angels will ascend and descend unhindered. Multitudes from diverse nationalities and ethnic groups will receive direct revelations of Jesus Christ through dreams and visions. Then, a mighty tidal wave of Holy Spirit revival will sweep across the world. Millions upon millions will be saved, delivered, and swept into the Kingdom of God.

CATACLYSMIC CONFRONTATION

"And war broke out in heaven: Michael and his angels fought against the dragon; and the dragon and his angels fought, but they did not prevail, nor was a place found for them in heaven any longer" *(Rev 12:7-8).*

The above scriptures speak of a war that broke out in heaven. Michael and his angels fought against satan and his fallen angels. Satan and his cohorts lost and were cast to the earth. On earth, Jesus defeated satan once again. We must remember, therefore, that satan is already a defeated foe!

Note that when satan lost the war in heaven, he was cast down to earth. Unable to come directly against God, the devil seeks to attack His creatures. The world we are living in has been turned into a spiritual battleground. Fierce and unrelenting battles are raging everyday over the hearts, minds, and souls of men. Whether you like it or not, you are involved in this conflict. No one is neutral—you are either for Christ or against Him. On the battleground there will be wounds, pain, bloodshed, and even death. Yes, there may be casualties and some may even stop serving the Lord. It is easy to be a quitter but God wants us to be overcomers. May we be like Shammah, one of David's mighty men, who did not flee from the heat of the battle:

"And after him was Shammah the son of Agee the Hararite. The Philistines had gathered together into a troop where there was a piece of ground full of lentils. Then the people fled from the Philistines.

But he stationed himself in the middle of the field, defended it, and killed the Philistines. And the Lord brought about a great victory" (2 Sam 23:11-12).

We wrestle against principalities, against powers, against the rulers of the darkness of this age, against spiritual hosts of wickedness in the heavenly places. To win life's spiritual battles, we are exhorted to be strong in the Lord and in the power of His might. We are to put on the complete armour of God, use the sword of the Spirit, which is the Word of God and to pray always.

Dr Morris Cerullo says that the majority of Christians presently are not prepared for the great spiritual confrontation that is soon going to take place in the world. He therefore urges Christians to get ready.

"For the devil has come down to you, having great wrath, because he knows that he has a short time" (Rev 12:12).

The Holy Spirit has not left the Church of Jesus Christ unprepared for the spiritual warfare ahead. Rather, He is equipping the people of God with a new anointing and inspiring new vigour, zeal, boldness, and holy aggression.

"the violent take it by force..." (Matt 11:12).

You might have noticed that an unusual number of books and songs on spiritual warfare have been written and sung lately. The Holy Spirit is the one inspiring it. He is preparing Spirit-filled believers mentally, emotionally, and spiritually to triumph over and defeat the powers of darkness.

He is preparing Spirit-filled believers mentally, emotionally, and spiritually to triumph over and defeat the powers of darkness.

SPIRITUAL WARFARE AND COVERINGS

*"then the Lord will create above every dwelling place of Mount Zion, and above her assemblies, a cloud and smoke by day and the shining of a flaming fire by night. For over all the glory there will be a **covering**. And there will be a tabernacle for **shade** in the daytime from the heat, for a place of **refuge**, and for a **shelter** from storm and rain" (Isa 4:5-6).*

When we engage in spiritual warfare, it is most essential to have spiritual coverings. Without it, we are exposed and vulnerable to the fiery darts of the enemy. Many believers and ministers of the gospel have become casualties because they failed to secure adequate covering over their lives and ministries. The enemy is always seeking to incapacitate us. If we do not have spiritual covering, we are easy targets indeed. In Exodus 26:1-14 and 36:8-19, we read about the four layers of coverings over the sanctuary of the tabernacle. Every believer is likened to the tabernacle and temple in which the Spirit of God dwells (Rom 8:9; 1 Cor 3:16; 6:19; 2 Cor 6:16).

The innermost layer of the tabernacle coverings is made of fine linen with figures of cherubim skillfully embroidered on it. The fine linen speaks of righteousness (Rev 19:8). According to Ephesians 6:14 and Isaiah 59:17, righteousness is like the protective breastplate that covers the body. "For He put on righteousness as a breastplate..." (Isa 59:17). The breastplate is a most important piece of armour as it protects the vital organs in the body, such as the heart, lungs and stomach. When you put on righteousness in your life, you are putting on an impenetrable piece of armour. The prince of this world has nothing to claim in Jesus, because He is righteous (John 14:30, 1 John 2:1). Therefore, the devil had no power over Him. However, with those Christians (especially leaders) who do not have righteousness in their lives and conduct, it is just a matter of time before the enemy gives them the T.K.O!

The cherubim speaks of the angelic covering God provides for us (Ps 34:7; 91:11). Angels are assigned to protect us. When a believer sins wilfully and fails to repent, he may lose this angelic covering. Once this happens, the believer can easily come under oppression from the enemy. However, this covering can be restored if the believer repents and walks in the fear of God once again.

The second layer of the tabernacle coverings is made of goat's hair. This speaks of the sin offerings. It draws our attention to the importance of making things right with God. The person who sins should make confession and repent immediately. Otherwise the devil, who is called the accuser, will find a weak point to attack (Rev 12:10).

"If we say that we have no sin, we deceive ourselves, and the truth is not in us. If we confess our sins, He is faithful and just to forgive us our sins and to cleanse us from all unrighteousness" (1 John 1:8-9). A humble and repentant heart will deliver us from the many wicked schemes of the evil one.

The third layer of the tabernacle coverings comprises ram's skin, dyed red. This speaks of the sacrifice of Jesus (Gen 22:13) and the power of His blood to protect us. "Now the blood shall be a sign for you on the houses where you are. And when I see the blood, I will pass over you; and the plague shall not be on you to destroy you when I strike the land of Egypt" (Exo 12:13). The destroying angel had to pass over the houses that were covered by the blood of the Lamb.

The fourth and outermost layer of the tabernacle coverings is made of badger's skin. This tough covering shields the sanctuary from the elements - the rain, wind, sun, and sand of the desert. This covering is likened to our faith in Jesus. Ephesians 6:16 says, "Above all, taking the shield of faith with which you will be able to quench all the fiery darts of the wicked one."

Just as the badger's skin formed the outermost layer of protection for the sanctuary, the shield constituted the first layer of protection for the soldiers of the past. The shield is indispensable because it is the main defence against arrows, sling-shots, javelins, spears and blows of the sword. Satan viciously attacked Job's property, family, health, character, and his relationship with God. He threw everything against Job. However, he could not break Job's faith in God. When everything else gave way, Job's faith prevailed (Job 13:15)! After Job was severely tried in the furnace of afflictions, he came forth as gold (Job 23:10).

I believe God is saying to us through the four coverings of the tabernacle, that we need at least four levels or layers of spiritual covering in order to have full protection. Without it, we can be easily 'hit' by the enemy in the battlefield of life.

There are also other important coverings besides the coverings of righteousness, angels, repentance, the blood of the Lamb, and faith. We can be covered by prayer and intercession. When we submit and make ourselves accountable to those that God has placed over us, we are protecting ourselves. The presence of God is a strong defence as well (Ps 91).

Make sure that you are well-covered spiritually. This is your most important and comprehensive 'life insurance policy'! Those who are not covered spiritually, or are only partly covered, fall easy prey to the devil's subtle deception and relentless assaults. God has promised to do certain things for us but we too have to be responsible spiritually.

"O God the Lord, the strength of my salvation, You have covered my head in the day of battle" (Ps 140:7).

JEHOVAH NISSI

"And Moses built an altar and called its name, The-Lord-Is-My-Banner" (Exo 17:15).

The banners of the Lord are being raised! In this new move of the Spirit, there is a sudden proliferation of banners. A great number of churches are making and raising up the banners of the Lord. They are being used increasingly in festivals of praise and marches for Jesus on the streets. God gets His people to do symbolically what He will do in reality. For in the spirit realm, His battle standard is being lifted up!

These banners are highly visible prophetic signs of the Spirit today! As in the natural, so it is happening in the spirit world.

"first...the natural, and afterward the spiritual" (1 Cor 15:46).

"When the enemy shall come in like a flood, the Spirit of the Lord will lift up a standard against him and put him to flight" (Isa 59:19 Amplified Bible).

These banners are prophetic signs that speak boldly and clearly. They make statements. Visible in the spirit realm as well, they are sending terror and panic to the demonic hosts. They know that the time of their judgment and punishment is near.

"'Their stronghold will fall because of terror; at sight of the battle standard (banner) their commanders will panic,' declares the Lord..." (Isa 31:9 NIV).

"awesome as an army with banners" (Song 6:4).

The banners are signs to the principalities and powers of darkness that:

1. Their dreaded judgment day draws near.
2. The mighty army of the Lord is being mustered and marshalled for battle (Isa 13:2-4).
3. The Lord of Hosts (Commander of Armies) is arising.
4. The Spirit of the Lord is determined to oppose the evil tide (Isa 59:19).

The banners are also prophetic signs to believers that:

1. Deliverance is at hand (Ps 60:4-5).
2. The battle belongs to the Lord.
3. We will triumph.
4. It is time to declare war in the heavenlies.
5. His banner over us is love (Song 2:4).

WEAPONS OF WARFARE

We do not wrestle against flesh and blood, but against principalities, against powers, against the rulers of the darkness of this age, against spiritual hosts of wickedness in the heavenly places. For though we walk in the flesh, we do not war in the flesh. The weapons of our warfare have divine power to destroy satanic strongholds. Some of the weapons we can wield in spiritual warfare are:

1. The name of Jesus (Phil 2:9-11).
2. The blood of the Lamb (Rev 12:11).

3. The Word of God (Eph 6:17).
4. Prayer (Eph 6:18).
5. Anointing (Isa 61:1-2).
6. Praise and worship (Ps 149:6-9).
7. Faith (Heb 11:33-34).
8. Fasting (Isa 58:6).
9. Gifts of the Spirit (1 Cor 12:1-11).
10. Praying in tongues (1 Cor 14:15).

The weapons of our warfare have divine power to destroy satanic strongholds.

When these spiritual weapons are executed by a body of believers who are united in spirit, the power released is vastly multiplied. There is power in agreement.

"Again I say to you that if two of you agree on earth concerning anything that they ask, it will be done for them by My Father in heaven" (Matt 18:19).

"Five of you shall chase a hundred, and a hundred of you shall put ten thousand to flight" (Lev 26:8).

Chapter 3

The Restoration Generation

1. David Recovered All

2. Jesus the Restorer

3. Repentance and Restoration

4. Restoration of Zion

5. Restoration of Apostles

6. Restoration of Angelic Activities (Ministries)

7. Restoration of Wealth and Prosperity

8. Restoration of Dance

LION OF JUDAH

DAVID RECOVERED ALL

Ziglag was one of the bases used by David. Once, while David and his men were away from Ziglag, the Amalekites invaded the defenceless village, razed it to the ground, and took all the inhabitants captive. When David returned to Ziglag, he discovered to his dismay what had happened. However, in his distress, he sought the Lord. The Lord encouraged David to **pursue** the Amalekites and assured him that he would without fail recover all. Therefore, David and his men went in hot pursuit. Finally, when they caught up with them, David and his men attacked the Amalekites. Amazingly, David and his men recovered all that the Amalekites had taken away, just as the Lord had said. "**So David recovered all** that the Amalekites had carried away, and David rescued his two wives. And nothing of theirs was lacking, either small or great, sons or daughters, spoil or anything which they had taken from them; **David recovered all**" (1 Sam 30:18-19).

David recovered all! This Davidic Generation will be a generation that **pursues** and **recovers all** just as David did. **This generation is The Restoration Generation.**

We are seeing the recognition and restoration of the Holy Spirit's Lordship in the Church. The gifts of the Spirit and especially the ministry gifts of the apostles and prophets are being restored to the Church. We are also seeing signs, wonders and miracles being restored. The recovery and restoration encompasses the arts and music, spiritual knowledge, prosperity and the role of the laity. God is restoring **all** things to the church. In this chapter on The Restoration Generation, I will touch on some of them.

David recovered all! This Davidic Generation will be a generation that pursues and recovers all just as David did. This generation is The Restoration Generation.

JESUS THE RESTORER

*"Whom heaven must receive until **the times of restoration of all things**, which God has spoken by the mouth of all His holy prophets since the world began" (Acts 3:21).*

The Greek word for restoration is *apokatastasis*. It relates to the restoration of a thing to its former condition. The Hebrew word for it is *schuwb*, meaning to turn back, to return. The basic meaning for *schuwb* is movement back to the point of departure.

Adam and Eve were made in the wonderful image of God. In the beginning they were innocent, immortal, and given dominion over the creatures of the earth. They also enjoyed sweet fellowship with God. However, when they fell into sin, they were no longer immortal. Sin consciousness came in and they experienced shame, guilt, and fear. They lost their spiritual authority and dominion over the creatures and their sweet fellowship with God was broken. Subsequently, sin entered the whole human race through them.

However, God in His foreknowledge, great mercy and compassion has provided for the restoration of fallen mankind.

"the Lamb slain from the foundation of the world" *(Rev 13:8).*

Jesus came and accomplished the greatest work of restoration when He died for our sins. The atoning work of Jesus at Calvary made it possible for us to be restored to the image of God. When on the cross Jesus cried, "It is finished," it meant that all that was required to be done for our reconciliation and full restoration was completed and made possible. On our part, we have to actively appropriate it by faith.

The atoning work of Jesus at Calvary made it possible for us to be restored to the image of God.

"Behold! The Lamb of God who takes away the sin of the world!" (John 1:29).

"Christ has redeemed us..." (Gal 3:13).

REPENTANCE AND RESTORATION

"He restores my soul..." (Ps 23:3).

The first essential step to restoration is repentance. It leads to restoration and opens the way for God to work anew in our lives. When we humble ourselves in repentance, God gives us grace for "God resists the proud, but gives grace to the humble" (1 Pet 5:5). Repentance may involve private or public confession. "Confess your trespasses to one another, and pray for one another, that you may be healed..." (James 5:15).

"And the son said to him, 'Father, I have sinned against heaven and in your sight, and am no longer worthy to be called your son...'" (Luke 15:21).

It involves a genuine change of mind and life's direction. As God's intention is to restore us "...till we all come...to a perfect man, to the measure of the stature of the fullness of Christ..." (Eph 4:13), we need to adjust our lives continually through constant and instant repentance. God's goal for us is the measure of the stature of the fullness of Christ—the Perfect Man.

We ought to repent of anything that is not Christ-like in our lives, and ask God to help us to be more like Jesus. Repentance leads to restoration.

RESTORATION OF ZION

Zion in the Bible is referred to literally and symbolically as:

1. A hill (Ps 2:6).
2. Jerusalem (2 Sam 5:6-9).
3. The Church, people of God (Heb 12:22-23).
4. Heaven (Rev 14:1).

The Lord has given me insight and precious revelation from the book of Lamentations concerning Zion. In this book, the prophet Jeremiah lamented the destruction and devastation of Zion. The once glorious and beautiful city of God became desolate.

The same can be said of the Church. She has been ravaged and made desolate by the enemy. But no more! God is in the process of restoring Zion, His Church, His Bride! Ezra, Nehemiah and Haggai are 'restoration-theme' books in the Bible.

Contrasted below is the destruction of Zion as found in the book of Lamentations and her restoration as spoken of in other scriptures.

Destruction of Zion	**Restoration of Zion**
1. Lonely *(Lam 1:1)*	1. Great throng/ multitude *(Jer 31:8)*
2. Slavery *(Lam 1:1)*	2. Liberty *(Jer 31:23)*
3. Bitter weeping *(Lam 1:2)*	3. Rejoicing *(Jer 31:13)*
4. None to comfort *(Lam 1:2)*	4. The Comforter has come *(John 14:16)*

Destruction of Zion   Restoration of Zion

Destruction of Zion	Restoration of Zion
5. Captivity (Lam 1:3)	5. Liberty (Ps 126:1)
6. No one comes to the set feasts (Lam 1:4)	6. Feasting in His presence once again (Jer 31:12,14)
7. Splendour has departed (Lam 1:6)	7. Adorning of the Bride (Isa 61:10)
8. Nakedness and shame (Lam 1:8)	8. Clothed with garments of salvation and the robe of righteousness (Isa 61:10)
9. Prophets have no vision from the Lord (Lam 2:9)	9. Sons and daughters shall prophesy, old men shall dream dreams (Joel 2:28)
10. Gird with sackcloth (Lam 2:10)	10. Put on beautiful garments (Isa 52:1)
11. Cessation of music (Lam 5:14)	11. Music, musical instruments restored (Ps 150)
12. Cessation of dance (Lam 5:15)	12. Dance restored (Jer 31:4)
13. Crown has fallen from the head (Lam 5:16)	13. Crowned with glory and honor (Heb 2:7)
14. Faint heart (Lam 5:17)	14. Revival (Isa 61:3)

Destruction of Zion	**Restoration of Zion**
15. Eyes grow dim *(Lam 5:17)*	15. Vision *(Joel 2:28)*
16. Desolate *(Lam 5:18)*	16. No desolation *(1sa 62:4)*

It is said of Kathryn Kuhlman that she wanted very much to live longer, so that she could witness the wonderful restoration and outpouring of God's Spirit in these end-times.

In this Restoration Generation, multitudes will be swept into the Kingdom of God. Services in the churches that are moving with the Spirit of God will be characterised by great liberty, celebration and joyful praise. The time to adorn the bride of Christ with spiritual gifts and grace is here. Many shall prophesy and see visions.

Music in the house of the Lord will be restored and will increase. Dancing before the Lord will be part of the worship service. The Lord will be the lifter of our heads, there will be revival breaking forth in many places. God will manifest Himself with greater glory in the midst of His people.

RESTORATION OF APOSTLES

*"And He Himself gave some to be **apostles...**"* *(Eph 4:11).*

The Church has been greatly blessed by the restoration of prophets and prophetic ministries. It seems that God has kept the good wine until now. If the restoration of prophets is exciting, the restoration of apostles will be even more so!

An apostle (*apostolos* in Greek) is one who is sent forth, one who is authorised by God Himself. It is a New Testament office instituted by Christ. Whereas most of the Old Testament Scriptures were written by prophets, the New Testament was written mainly by apostles. Together with the prophets, the apostles represent the foundational ministry of the Church (Eph 2:19-20). The apostles and apostolic ministries have been in existence for a long time. There is a difference however, in this new wave of restoration. Thousands of apostles who are indeed apostles in their spirit and calling are arising. They are already here! The full manifestation of their calling, office, and gifts is at hand. Their unveiling is near.

"Paul, called to be an apostle of Jesus Christ..." (1 Cor 1:1). "Then after fourteen years..." (Gal 2:1).

All apostles must have a definite call. Paul was called to be an apostle after his encounter with the Lord on the road to Damascus (Acts 9:1-18). But his actual commissioning only took place about fourteen years later! Like the prophets, God prepares the apostles in a unique way. The testings, tempering and moulding processes are beyond the ordinary. Generally, we find that the apostles and prophets are the most persecuted lot, because they pose the greatest threat to the kingdom of darkness. These two ministries, being revelational in nature, have the ability to discern and expose the work of the enemy.

a. Examples of Apostles and Apostolic Ministries

An example is Hudson Taylor who pioneered the China Inland Mission, now called the Overseas Missionary Fellowship. Another example is Smith Wigglesworth who was known to have raised up to fourteen people from the dead by his faith and prevailing prayer which laid hold of heaven's power. Dr David Yonggi Cho who has established the largest church in the history of Christendom is another modern day apostle. There are also apostolic prophets and apostolic evangelists.

A great number of apostles are on the rise—apostles who are prepared and anointed by God for this time and hour in history. Their ministries in this Davidic Generation will greatly contribute towards the global harvest of souls.

b. Work of an Apostle

1. Equipping the saints for the work of ministry (Eph 4:12).
2. Calling forth ministries and positioning people.
3. Breaking new ground (pioneering) in various fields.
4. Planting and establishing churches.
5. Spiritual father (mentoring), e.g. Paul to Timothy.
6. Missions and relief aid (Acts 11:29-30).
7. Establishing new ministries - foundation (Eph 2:20).
8. Disciplining, correcting and providing a balanced view (Gal 2:11-13; Acts 15:36-41).
9. Making major decisions regarding churches (2 Cor 11:28; Acts 15:1-11).

c. Other Marks of an Apostle

1. Spiritual authority.
2. Wisdom.
3. Extended ministry (beyond one's own church).
4. Master builder - ability to build lives, ministries, and churches (1 Cor 3:10).
5. Ability to govern (put things in order).

d. Tests of an Apostle

"And you have tested those who say they are apostles and are not, and have found them liars" (Rev 2:2).

Just as there are false prophets, there are also false apostles claiming to be what they are not. True apostles are identified by:

1. Their love for the church of Jesus Christ.
2. The fruits of their ministry (Matt 7:15-20).
3. Their walk with God.
4. The signs and wonders in their ministry (2 Cor 12:12).
5. Their capabilities in revelatory flow (Gal 1:12; 2:2).
6. The anointing in their lives.
7. Recognition from other apostles and prophets.
8. Humility and sacrifice.

These characteristics would testify to their credentials, calling and office.

Like prophets, apostles are capable of revelational knowledge.

*"how that by **revelation** He made known to me the mystery (as I wrote before in a few words, by which, when you read, you may understand my knowledge in the mystery of Christ), which in other ages was not made known to the sons of men, as it has now been **revealed** by the Spirit to His holy apostles and prophets..."* (Eph 3:3-5).

*"For I neither received it from man, nor was I taught it, but it came through the **revelation** of Jesus Christ"* (Gal 1:12).

Apostles also contribute balance and stability to the prophetic ministries.

"If anyone thinks himself to be a prophet or spiritual, let him acknowledge that the things which I write to you are the commandments of the Lord" (1 Cor 14:37).

RESTORATION OF ANGELIC ACTIVITIES (MINISTRIES)

"The angel of the Lord encamps all around those who fear Him, and delivers them" (Ps 34:7).

There are almost 300 references to angels in the Bible. In this Restoration Generation, there will be an increase in angelic activities (ministries) and blessed interventions in the lives of those who love the Lord, just as in Bible days. There are numerous references to angelic activities in the book of Acts alone (Acts 1:9-11; 5:17-20; 7:30, 35, 38; 8:26; 10:1-7, 22; 11:13; 12:5-7, 23; 27:23).

This increase in angelic activities also serves to counter the increase in demonic activities in this end-time (Rev 12:12). We need to understand the ministry of holy angels anew to better co-operate with them.

During the course of my ministry, there have been several blessed angelic visitations and manifestations in our church services. Whenever this has happened, the services have been very unusual and glorious. I would like to briefly recall one such meeting where there was angelic visitation and manifestation.

Angelic Visitation

"With open eyes, you shall see the glory of God! With open eyes, you shall see the glory of God!" Each time I prophesied these words, they rose stronger from within my spirit. I must have prophesied these words at least five times during a water baptism gathering (in the Golden Sands Baptist Centre beach house) at Port Dickson.

Two weeks later it happened. About ten of us had just returned from a blessed seminar in Singapore that was conducted by an anointed prophet of God. We headed straight back to church for the Intercessors' Meeting that Friday evening. As we worshipped Him at the start of the meeting, the atmosphere was electrifying. We felt the awesome, holy presence of God in our midst—the kind of awesomeness that fills me with reverential fear and causes an inner trembling. Rising continually from my spirit were these words "We revere You, Holy

Lord; we revere You, Holy Lord." There was a dense anointing in the air. We continued to worship with a deep inner reverence for quite a while, savouring and soaking in His presence.

As was customary, I tried to teach from the Bible. However, it was a rather inappropriate thing for me to do that particular evening. I soon realised that those present were no longer paying attention to me. I saw the look of astonished wonderment on some of their faces. Some of them were nudging and talking to their neighbours in hushed but excited whispers. I noticed that they were looking past me and a few were pointing to the stage just behind me. When I asked if they were seeing angels, they nodded in affirmation. The teaching session that evening ended abruptly!

I told the members that we would not have the usual prayer meeting. I directed all of them to kneel at the altar area skirting the stage. As we continued to worship, one of the members, Christine, saw the angels moving down from the stage. She quickly grabbed a microphone and began to describe what she was seeing in excited tones. Two angels were ministering to each worshipper. As fast as she could, Christine also interpreted what it was the angels were ministering to each individual.

Immediately after the meeting ended, the members excitedly affirmed all that Christine had seen and described. She had accurately described what the angels had brought to each individual in answer to their prayers. The amazing thing is no one knew of the individual's prayer except the Lord. For example, my wife, Irene, was praying for her lips to be cleansed and Christine saw an angel bring a burning coal towards her (Isa 6:5-7). She also saw two robes placed upon me as I knelt in prayer and gave the interpretation concerning the significance of the robes. They were robes of righteousness and authority. I took advantage of the nearness of the Lord's presence to pour my heart out before Him. Heaven seemed so blissfully close that night. Just imagine how excited we were, experiencing something so extraordinary.

That evening, the meeting was longer than usual and I closed the meeting about three and a half hours later, around 11.30 pm. That was probably another inappropriate thing which I did. In retrospect, I realised I should have continued the meeting. They told me the angels were still around when we were leaving the church. My wife saw the 'main one', who was bigger and taller than the others, standing behind the pulpit. He was about seven and a half feet tall; the others were of human height. About eight church members saw the angels with open eyes that night.

The powerful effects of God's presence and anointing were still felt even as we had supper later on. I distinctly remember how we showed the goose pimples on our hands to one another as we sat at the hawker stall. Many of us could not sleep till the early hours of the morning. Our whole beings were so charged, quickened and energized. Much praise and thanksgiving ascended to God for that wonderful visitation and the blessings we received.

RESTORATION OF WEALTH AND PROSPERITY

"That I may cause those who love me to inherit wealth, that I may fill their treasuries" (Pro 8:21).

"And also the nation whom they serve I will judge; afterward they shall come out with great possessions" (Gen 15:14).

"And you shall remember the Lord your God, for it is He who gives you power to get wealth..." (Deut 8:18).

The Scriptures speak of the times of restoration of **all** things. This includes wealth and prosperity. Laying aside extreme emphases, the recent teachings concerning wealth and prosperity have a valid place in the Word of God. When the scriptural teaching on this subject is properly understood, it can trigger off cycles of sowing and harvesting of finances. Churches and ministries will also experience a greater release of finances and resources.

During this season of restoration, we need the kind of wisdom God gave to Joseph in the book of Genesis - the wisdom to accumulate and manage financial resources. Joseph was more powerful during the seven years of famine than he was during the seven years of plenty because he acted upon the revelation he received.

Soon God will judge the god that this world is currently worshipping - MAMMON! The economic and monetary system of this world (The Babylonian System) is heading towards breakdown. The BIG

CRASH is inevitable. God, in His merciful providence, will allow it to happen so that the populace of this world will turn from worshipping this great big idol.

"And the merchants of the earth will weep and mourn over her, for no one buys their merchandise anymore: merchandise of gold and silver, precious stones and pearls, fine linen and purple, silk and scarlet, every kind of citron wood, every kind of object of ivory, every kind of object of most precious wood, bronze, iron, and marble; and cinnamon and incense, fragrant oil and frankincense, wine and oil, fine flour and wheat, cattle and sheep, horses and chariots, and bodies and souls of men. And the fruit that your soul longed for has gone from you, and all the things which are rich and splendid have gone from you, and you shall find them no more at all. The merchants of these things, who became rich by her, will stand at a distance for fear of her torment, weeping and wailing, and saying, 'Alas, alas, that great city that was clothed in fine linen, purple, and scarlet, and adorned with gold and precious stones and pearls! For in one hour such great riches came to nothing.' And every shipmaster, all who travel by ship, sailors, and as many as trade on the sea, stood at a distance and cried out when they saw the smoke of her burning, saying, 'What is like this great city?' And they threw dust on their heads and cried out, weeping and wailing, and saying, 'Alas, alas, that great city, in which all who had ships on the sea became rich by her wealth! For in one hour she is made desolate'" (Rev 18:11-19).

May we have the prophetic wisdom of Joseph to prepare for this eventuality - the present restoration of wealth and prosperity and the coming 'lean' years!

"So the advice was good in the eyes of Pharoah...You shall be over my house, and all my people shall be ruled according to your word...So he gathered up all the food of the seven years...and laid up the food in the cities... Joseph gathered very much grain...The famine was in all lands, but in all the land of Egypt there was bread...So all countries came to Joseph in Egypt to buy grain..." (Gen 41:37-57).

Different Kinds of Power

There are different kinds and forms of power. There is the power of knowledge. With the right scientific knowledge, nuclear bombs can be made, more powerful computers invented, etc. We are well aware of the "people's power" - the power of the masses. There are also political, economic, and military powers. Manipulative power play and rivalry go on all the time in this world. The different forms of power mentioned above affect and control our lives to some degree—almost completely, in some lives.

Besides these 'natural' forms of power, there are spiritual powers (Eph 6:12). The ultimate power above all powers is God! He is omnipotent - all powerful!

Wealth – A Form of Power

Money was devised by man as a medium of

exchange. By itself it is amoral. It is the love of money that is the root of all kinds of evil (1 Tim 6:10). Wealth can be our master or servant. When it controls us, we are reduced to becoming its slave. When we make it our servant, it becomes a blessing to us and others. When God puts wealth into our hands, He is giving us the power to bless. It is given for the furtherance of the Gospel and the end-time harvest of souls. In Genesis, Joseph was more powerful during the seven years of famine than during the seven years of plenty. And just like Joseph, this end-time Davidic Generation will have greater power of influence when the world's economic system collapses and the lean years follow. It is for these main reasons that God is restoring wealth and prosperity to His people in this Davidic Generation. The release of finances is an important key to this end-time harvest.

God is causing a great financial release to come to His people so that the task of spreading the Gospel will be speeded up. We are in a race against time. There will be an increase in missions emphasis. We will see missions giving and activities multiplied.

The Principle of Seedtime and Harvest

"While the earth remains, seedtime and harvest...shall not cease" (Gen 8:22).

"Give, and it will be given to you: good measure...will be put into your bosom..." (Luke 6:38).

Many who have believed and acted upon the Word of God in respect to giving have testified that it works! Personally, I have many good testimonies in this area of sowing and reaping finances. The blessings that return to us may come in many forms. It is not limited to financial returns alone. It may take the form of divine protection, healing, revelation, favour, or prosperity in our spirit and soul.

We must learn to give, give and give until the spirit of poverty (that constant nagging fear of insufficiency and not having enough) is broken. King David was a great giver. He would not offer to God anything that costs him nothing (2 Sam 24:24).

*"Now for the house of my God I have prepared with all my might: gold for things to be made of gold, silver for things of silver, bronze for things of bronze, iron for things of iron, wood for things of wood, onyx stones, stones to be set, glistening stones of various colors, all kinds of precious stones, and marble slabs in abundance. Moreover, because I have set my affection on the house of my God, I have given to the house of my God, **over and above all that I have prepared for the holy house, my own special treasure of gold and silver**"* (1 Chron 29:2-3).

When we give liberally, a number of things may happen:

1. We develop in the grace of giving (2 Cor 8:2).
2. We minister to the saints (2 Cor 8:4).
3. We reap from what we sow (2 Cor 8:6).
4. We supply to those who lack (2 Cor 8:14).

5. We prove our love (2 Cor 8:24).
6. God's grace abounds towards us (2 Cor 9:8).
7. God supplies and multiplies the seed sown and increases the fruit of our righteousness (2 Cor 9:10).
8. We cause thanksgiving to ascend to God (2 Cor 9:11-12).
9. We supply the needs of the saints (2 Cor 9:12).
10. God is glorified (2 Cor 9:13).
11. We receive prayer and blessings from the recipients of the gift (2 Cor 9:14).

"Freely you have received, freely give" (Matt 10:8).

RESTORATION OF DANCE

*"You shall again be adorned with your tambourines, and shall go forth in the **dances** of those who rejoice"* (Jer 31:4).

*"Then shall the virgin rejoice in the **dance**, and the young men and the old, together; for I will turn their mourning to joy, will comfort them, and make them rejoice rather than sorrow"* (Jer 31:13).

*"Let them praise His name with the **dance**; let them sing praises to Him with the timbrel and harp"* (Ps 149:3).

*"Praise Him with the timbrel and the **dance**; praise Him with stringed instruments and flutes!"* (Ps 150:4).

Little children do not just walk. It is natural for them to hop, skip, jump, run, wiggle and dance. They are natural and free in expressing themselves. This is what God intended us to be: natural, free and full of life. Where there is life, there are movements. Life and freedom are best expressed through dance movements. "For in Him we **live** and **move** and have our being..." (Acts 17:28).

There is a restoration of dance in churches and it is picking up strong momentum, catching on and spreading fast in many nations of the world. Dance troupes are flourishing in many churches. Christians are showing keen interest in this expressive form of worship.

The restoration of the dance is another prophetic sign of the end-time spiritual revival and harvest. It is an indication that the Feast of Tabernacles is upon us! The word feast in Hebrew is *chagag* which also means to dance. One main characteristic of the Feast of Tabernacles is rejoicing through dance.

The restoration of the dance is another prophetic sign of the end-time spiritual revival and harvest.

"You have turned for me my mourning into dancing..." (Ps 30:11).

"you shall rejoice before the Lord your God for seven days." (Lev 23:40).

In this end-time, God is using the powerful dynamics of dance to liberate His people physically, emotionally, and spiritually from crippling inhibitions, fears and self-consciousness. He is bringing them into the glorious liberty that belongs to the children of God.

Anointed dancers release the life and liberty of God. This spiritual release and expression directly counters the spirit of heaviness and bondage. The life and anointing released through dance can also help to free people who are stifled and bound. Rejoicing in faith through dance is powerful. The whole atmosphere in a church service can be liberated and changed through the faith exercised and anointing released through the dance. Pastors and church elders who encourage the development of such a dance ministry in their churches will see their church services more blessed, liberated, and joyful.

In this end-time, God is using the powerful dynamics of dance to liberate His people physically, emotionally, and spiritually from crippling inhibitions, fears and self-consciousness.

Dance is body language. It is a highly visual and powerful means of communication. You will have witnessed in various media how sensuality can be communicated just through certain movements and gestures. In contrast, through appropriate dance movements; praise, worship, love and joy can be portrayed and expressed.

"You shall love the Lord your God with all your heart, with all your soul, and with all your might" *(Deut 6:5).*

We are to love God with all of our being - spirit, soul and body. Dance is one of the ways through which we can express our love to Him with our whole being. Artists express themselves through colours, musicians through their instruments and singers through their voices. Dancers express themselves through movement.

There are many types of dance:

a. Dance of victory/deliverance   - Exo 15:20
b. Dancing before the Lord   - 2 Sam 6:14
c. Festival dances   - Jdg 21:19-21
d. Dance of rejoicing   - Jer 31:13
e. Worship dance   - Ps 149:3
f. Warfare dance (tambourines)   - Isa 30:32
g. Prophetic dance   - 1 Sam 18:7
h. Social/cultural dance   - Job 21:11

Because dance is an expression of the person, the dancer must first be a worshipper to be able to express the depths of his/her relationship with the Lord. Techniques are secondary. The Father seeks those who worship Him in spirit and in truth.

Since dance is highly visual and involves bodily movement, standards must be set and observed by those who desire to be involved in this particular ministry in a local church:

1. Be modest in dressing. Avoid figure hugging clothings, sleeveless blouses, short and tight skirts, low necklines or anything that will distract the congregation from worshipping the Lord.

2. Make appropriate movements. While no defined style of dance movements are given in the Scriptures, any movements that are suggestive and sensual and draw attention to the dancer's anatomy are to be avoided.

3. Be a worshipper and be disciplined in personal devotion.

4. Be faithful and committed to the local church.

5. Be submissive to the church's leadership.

6. Be willing to sacrifice time for rehearsals and finances for costumes.

Chapter 4

The Prophetic Generation

1. David the Prophet
2. Prophets, Watchmen and Trumpets
3. Different Kinds of Prophet
4. Blessed Solitude
5. Prophets and Eagles
6. Eagle's Eyes
7. Heavenly Places
8. Value of Prophecy
9. God Speaks to Us in Many Ways

DAVID THE PROPHET

"David...therefore, being a **prophet***..." (Acts 2:29-30).*

"the Holy Spirit spoke before by the mouth of David..." (Acts 1:16).

"The Spirit of the Lord spoke by me, and His Word was on my tongue" (2 Sam 23:2).

According to Scripture, David was a prophet. In fact, he ranks amongst the great prophets of the Bible. Prophecies flow richly in many of his psalms. His prophecies concerning the Messiah are amazingly accurate and detailed. A prime example is Psalm 22. Only a prophet could receive such a tremendous amount of detailed revelation that David did. Altogether, he wrote more than 200 verses of prophecy. The prophetic anointing is a significant characteristic of his life.

The Spirit of the Lord was upon David (1 Sam 16:13). The Lord was constantly with him (1 Sam 16:18; 18:12, 14, 28; 2 Sam 5:10; 7:9). He habitually inquired of the Lord (1 Sam 23:2, 4; 30:8; 2 Sam 5:19, 23). Some of these factors are important keys in the life of David as a prophet.

This present generation, like David, is a Prophetic Generation. In this generation, the prophets and the prophetic ministries are being restored to the church in an intensive and extensive measure that has never been seen before. We will witness again the power of the prophets. As in the lives of Samuel, Elijah and

Elisha, the supernatural power of the prophetic mantle will be demonstrated through signs, wonders and miracles. The end-time church will be a prophetic church. Those who are in the flow of this present move of God will be a prophetic people— **The Prophetic Generation.**

"And they shall prophesy" (Acts 2:18).

PROPHETS, WATCHMEN AND TRUMPETS

"Cry aloud, spare not; lift up your voice like a ***trumpet****; tell My people their transgression, and the house of Jacob their sins" (Isa 58:1).*

In the Scriptures, two main types of trumpet are used. They are the silver trumpet and the *shophar*, which is made from ram's horn. These instruments produce a loud and distinct sound which can be heard from afar. In Numbers chapter 10, the trumpets were used:

1. for calling the assembly of leaders and the congregation (Num 10:2-7).
2. for directing the movements of the camp (Num 10:2, 5, 6).
3. to invoke the help of God during times of war (Num 10:9).
4. during the appointed feasts days and at the beginning of each month (Num 10:10).

In Scripture, the trumpet symbolises the prophetic voice. At times, this voice comes as a sudden BLAST that jolts the sleeping conscience awake! It may cause a gripping conviction in people's hearts. Some may want the prophetic voice to sound sweet like the flute or soothing like the pan pipes. But more often than not, the prophetic voice will be like the blaring horn. When prophets speak, though their voice may not actually sound loud to the ear, it thunders within the hearts of the hearers. The prophetic voice has a different timbre, it rings with the authority of "Thus saith the Lord".

The prophetic voice has a different timbre, it rings with the authority of "Thus saith the Lord".

"But His word was in my heart like a burning fire shut up in my bones; I was weary of holding it back, and I could not" (Jer 20:9).

This is not to say that prophets cannot minister with compassion and gentleness. However, there is an underlying zeal and passion that burns within the prophet's heart. Prophets have a passion to purify and perfect the saints. They will boldly speak and prophesy against evil and unrighteousness.

"And He found in the temple those who sold oxen and sheep and doves, and the moneychangers doing business. When He had made a whip of cords, He drove them all out of the temple, with the sheep and the oxen, and poured out the changers' money and overturned the tables. And He said to those who sold doves, 'Take these things away! Do not

*make My Father's house a house of merchandise!'
Then His disciples remembered that it was written,
'Zeal for Your house has eaten Me up'" (John 2:14-
17).*

Prophets minister with such accuracy that they either
receive a good response or strong reactions from the
people. When prophets preach, the people tend to
think, "He is talking about me again." Rejection
tends to be the prophets' lot. In Bible days, many of
them were persecuted and killed in attempts to
silence their voice.

**Rejection tends to be the prophets'
lot. In Bible days, many of them
were persecuted and killed in
attempts to silence their voice.**

---

*"When they heard these things they were cut to the
heart, and they gnashed at him with their teeth. But
he, being full of the Holy Spirit, gazed into heaven
and saw the glory of God, and Jesus standing at the
right hand of God, and said, 'Look! I see the heavens
opened and the Son of Man standing at the right
hand of God!' Then they cried out with a loud voice,
stopped their ears, and ran at him with one accord;
and they cast him out of the city and stoned him.
And the witnesses laid down their clothes at the feet
of a young man named Saul" (Acts 7:54-58).*

The trumpets of God will continue to sound the call

to repentance and restoration. They will continue to warn the people of danger, of the sin of idolatry and compromise. It is the 'burden' of the prophets to testify against sin and unrighteousness in the body of Christ even though this may be unpopular with some, especially those living in sin. For they are zealous to present to Christ a pure and unblemished Bride.

"For I am jealous for you with godly jealousy. For I have betrothed you to one husband, that I may present you as a chaste virgin to Christ" (2 Cor 11:2).

"Yet He sent prophets to them, to bring them back to the Lord; and they testified against them, but they would not listen" (2 Chron 24:19).

In Bible days, the watchmen of the cities were placed on duty, round the clock, day and night. Equipped with trumpets, they were positioned at strategic watchtowers on the high walls. Usually, they would be the first to detect enemy invasion and other impending danger. The watchmen's responsibility was to alert the inhabitants by sounding the alarm with their trumpets:

*"But if the **watchman** sees the sword coming and does not blow the **trumpet**, and the people are not warned, and the sword comes and takes any person from among them, he is taken away in his iniquity; but his blood I will require at the **watchman's** hand. So you, son of man: I have made you a **watchman** for the house of Israel; therefore you shall hear a word from My mouth and warn them for Me" (Eze 33:6-7).*

Prophets are likened unto the watchmen. **Being people that are more poised and keen in the spirit, they are usually the first to detect and discern the attack of the enemy.** For example, the prophet Elisha was able to frustrate the ambush manoeuvres of the king of Syria, through the revelations he received from God. "Now the king of Syria was making war against Israel; and he took counsel with his servants, saying, 'My camp will be in such and such a place.' And the man of God sent to the king of Israel, saying, 'Beware that you do not pass this place, for the Syrians are coming down there.' Then the king of Israel sent someone to the place of which the man of God had told him. Thus he warned him, and he was watchful there, not just once or twice" (2 Kgs 6:8-10).

Later, the upset and angry king of Syria sent a large army to capture Elisha at Dothan. That effort failed too! Prophets, because of their supernatural gifts and spiritual alertness, pose a major threat to the kingdom of darkness. They are able to know, at an early stage, deception, compromise and the dangers of missing the will of God. Thus, they are often the primary obstacles to and targets of the enemy.

Trumpets were used to direct the movement of the camp during the Israelites' journey in the wilderness. Prophets are the voice of God. They are sent forth preceding each new move of God. They help to prepare the people for the things God is doing in any particular spiritual season, just as John the Baptist was sent to prepare the way for Jesus:

"The voice of one crying in the wilderness: 'Prepare the way of the Lord; make straight in the desert a highway for our God" (Isa 40:3).

In the past, not many prophets had emerged. What we are now witnessing is totally unprecedented. A great big company of prophets has been raised and sent forth to prepare the way for the Lord. They number by the thousands. They are being sent forth to prepare the way for the greatest move of the Holy Spirit in these last days. The prophets are pointing the way and assisting the churches to move in the right direction.

DIFFERENT KINDS OF PROPHET

"And it shall come to pass in the last days, says God, that I will pour out of My Spirit on all flesh; your sons and your daughters shall prophesy, your young men shall see visions, your old men shall dream dreams. And on My menservants and on My maidservants I will pour out My spirit in those days; and they shall prophesy..." (Acts 2:17-18).

There are different types of prophet raised by the Lord to fulfill His diverse purposes. Prophets, at different stages of maturity, operate at varied levels of anointing and revelatory flow.

1. Naba (spontaneous) prophets - Haggai
2. Ro-eh (seer) prophets - Samuel, Ezekiel, Gad
3. Judge prophets - Deborah, Samuel
4. Scribe (write and teach) prophets - Nathan, Gad
5. Musician prophets - Chenaniah, David

6. Statesman prophets - Daniel, Isaiah, Nathan
7. Evangelist prophets - Isaiah
8. Weeping (intercessory) prophets - Jeremiah
9. Prophets of power - Elijah, Elisha
10. Apostolic prophets - Moses, Samuel

BLESSED SOLITUDE

"So the child grew and became strong in spirit, and was in the deserts till the day of his manifestation to Israel" (Luke 1:80).

Great eagles fly alone. Eagle Christians treasure solitude. For example, we read of Elijah being alone on top of Mount Carmel. Jesus often sought a solitary place and John the Baptist lived in a remote place. Prophets know the right time to appear publicly and when to withdraw from the crowd. **It is because of their unusual spiritual inclination that prophets are often misunderstood as being anti-social.**

Prophets live in two worlds. They listen to the natural and spirit worlds. They are conscious of both realms. The nature of their ministry is such that they require tremendous amounts of time to be alone with the Lord. It is through such times of being alone in prayer and waiting that their spirits are finely tuned, positioned and poised to hear from God. Therefore, prophets often seek to be alone. All the hustle and bustle of life will only distract them. They love the harmony that exists in nature. In this kind of environment, their inner consciousness is heightened, thus helping them to remain sharp in the spirit and receive 'first-hand' revelation.

"Surely I have calmed and quieted my soul..." (Ps 131:2).

PROPHETS AND EAGLES

"Behold, He shall come up and fly like the eagle, and spread His wings over Bozrah..." (Jer 49:22).

The eagle is king of the birds. Aloft in the sky and gliding gracefully with its wings spread out wide, the eagle is certainly a majestic sight. By observing the nature and ways of the eagle, we can learn many lessons concerning the prophetic ministry for there are many similarities between the nature of prophets and the nature of eagles.

"There are three things which are too wonderful for me, yes, four which I do not understand: The way of an eagle in the air..." (Pro 30:18-19).

The eagle has the strength of patience. It wisely waits for the breeze and utilises the power of the wind. It knows the optimum timing to mount up and ride the wind, or be borne by the rising thermal. I have seen eagles soaring for a long duration without having to flap their wings even once. It is just not an eagle's nature to flap its wings frantically and exhaust itself. The eagle is highly energy-efficient. More than flying, it soars. We are not able to see the wind but only feel the effects thereof. The eagle, on the other hand, can read and understand the wind's direction, current and speed.

Similarly, this Prophetic Generation is like the eagle. They are learning the secret of waiting upon the Lord. They will acquire the ability to know the appropriate and precise time to move with the Spirit of God. They will learn and understand more of the ways and flow of the Holy Spirit. Prophetic people do not strive and strain with unfruitful works of the flesh. They move in the Spirit and minister with effortless ease by utilising the power of the Holy Spirit. A mature prophetic people will be sensitive to the slightest movement of the Holy Spirit within them.

A mature prophetic people will be sensitive to the slightest movement of the Holy Spirit within them.

EAGLE'S EYES

The eagle's eyes are unique and remarkable. They have a double layer of eyelids. One set protects the eyes during swift dives. It also shields the eyes from strong winds and the glare of the sun. The muscles in the eagle's eyes allow for linear movement of the lens. This telescopic capability of its eyes enables the eagle to see small objects even from very great distances and heights. The eagle's field of vision is wide, up to 275 degrees.

Likewise, the Prophetic Generation will have the power of perception. Many in this generation will be able to see further and beyond the natural realm, right into the realm of the spirit. They will see visions, angels and other things of the Spirit *("I will pour out My Spirit...your young men shall see visions..." Joel 2:28)*. They will be able to see things afar off and prophesy about them before they happen. Their focus will be on the Lord, the author and finisher of their faith. They will be transformed into His image and likeness, from glory to glory, as they behold Him. "But we all, with unveiled face, beholding as in a mirror the glory of the Lord, are being transformed into the same image from glory to glory, just as by the Spirit of the Lord" (2 Cor 3:18).

"These things says the Son of God, who has eyes like a flame of fire..." (Rev 2:18).

The eyes of the eagle are bold, fierce and penetrating. The Prophetic Generation will be characterised by boldness. It will be a boldness that results from receiving the revelation of God. They will be a people who live in the "know".

The prophets may seem fierce at times. The fire of God within them can be seen in their eyes. Prophets have a passion to perfect and purify the saints. Prophets, being visionaries, see the ideal of God. They are intolerant of things that fall short of God's glory. One burden of prophets and an oft repeated theme is for the people of God to return to God's ideal. In the book of Jeremiah alone, the word, "return" *(shuwb)* occurs 111 times. Prophets will plead, exhort, and rebuke until the church returns to the "divine pattern".

"If you will return, O Israel," says the Lord, "Return to Me; and if you will put away your abominations out of My sight, then you shall not be moved" (Jer 4:1).

"Return, you backsliding children, and I will heal your backslidings" (Jer 3:22).

Like the eagle's eye that is penetrating, the Prophetic Generation will have the ability to discern. They will see through deception and they will perceive in the spirit quickly.

HEAVENLY PLACES

"Come up here, and I will show you things which must take place after this" (Rev 4:1).

"and raised us up together, and made us sit together in the heavenly places in Christ Jesus..." (Eph 2:6).

The eagle can fly higher than any other bird. Some species are capable of flying to a height of 25,000 feet! From this vantage point, the eagle sees far beyond the horizon and has a panoramic view. It is able to enjoy scenery and observe things that other birds and creatures may not experience. The eagle has "God's eye view". The eagle speaks of the heavenly nature. The Prophetic Generation will not settle for lowly, mediocre living or service. They will reach for the heights and seek to excel for the glory of God. They will learn to see things through the eyes of Christ and from God's perspective. They will have a wider and deeper understanding of the purposes of God. They will seek to be filled with all the fullness of God.

"that you may be filled with all the fullness of God" *(Eph 3:19).*

VALUE OF PROPHECY

Prophecy is essentially saying what God says!

"Where the word of a king is, there is power..." **(Ecc 8:4).**

Prophecy:
1. Encourages and strengthens (2 Chron 15:8).
2. Edifies (1 Cor 14:3).
3. Gives direction (1 Sam 10:2-8).
4. Helps people find their place in ministry (Acts 13:1-4).
5. Affirms and confirms (1 Sam 10:1-9).
6. Warns (Acts 21:10-11).
7. Exposes the enemy's plans (2 Kgs 6:8-12).
8. Helps you to wage a good warfare (1 Tim 1:18).
9. Unleashes miracles (2 Kgs 3:16-20).
10. Forth-tells (2 Kgs 13:14-19).
11. Fore-tells (2 Kgs 7:1, 16).
12. Changes a person's spirit and attitude (1 Sam 10:6).

GOD SPEAKS TO US IN MANY WAYS

"For God may speak in one way, or in another..." *(Job 33:14).*

"God, who at various times and in different ways spoke in time past to the fathers by the prophets" *(Heb 1:1).*

God speaks to us in many ways. Here are some of them:

1. All Bible Scripture

"All Scripture is given by inspiration of God, and is profitable for doctrine, for reproof, for correction, for instruction in righteousness" (2 Tim 3:16).

God speaks to us primarily through the Bible. It is His unchanging, inspired, and established Word. His divine nature, laws, eternal principles, and counsel are revealed in His Word. It is the divine standard and truth by which all things are judged. The most common way God speaks to us is through the Scriptures, yet it is also the most important way.

2. Specific scriptures quickened to us

"And He opened their understanding, that they might comprehend the Scriptures" (Luke 24:45).

The Holy Spirit may impress upon our hearts a particular verse or word from the Bible. This usually happens when we are reading it. And when this occurs, we should meditate on it to gain the full benefit.

3. Five-fold ministries

God also speaks to us through the ministries of the apostles, prophets, evangelists, pastors and teachers.

4. Still small voice within

"and after the earthquake a fire...and after the fire a still small voice..." (1 Kgs 19:12-13).

God's voice may come as a gentle prompting or quiet whisper within. One needs to be still and settled in the spirit to hear this still small voice.

5. Inner witness

"And the Holy Spirit also witnesses to us..." (Heb 10:15).

We can sense a 'yes' or 'no' within us. The Holy Spirit may give us warning or encouragement.

6. A song

"God my Maker, Who gives songs in the night..." (Job 35:10).

The Holy Spirit may inspire a song within us or bring it to our remembrance. He may speak to us through the lyrics of the song.

7. Impression

"Paul observing him intently and seeing that he had faith to be healed" (Acts 14:9).

Sometimes the impression may be strong; at other times, it may be faint. It may also come in the form of images.

8. Release or restraint in the spirit

"Now when they had gone through Phrygia and the region of Galatia, they were forbidden by the Holy Spirit to preach the word in Asia. After they had come to Mysia, they tried to go into Bithynia, but the Spirit did not permit them" (Acts 16:6-7).

The Holy Spirit will give you an inner release when you are moving in the right direction. You may sense an inner restraint if it is not. Check whether there is a flow in the spirit.

9. A spontaneous thought

Though it may come as a spontaneous thought, we are not to trust every thought that comes to mind. It needs to be sieved. A renewed mind will be a safeguard against error.

10. A rhema word

"for He will not speak on His own authority, but whatever He hears He will speak; and He will tell you things to come. He will glorify Me, for He will take of what is mine and declare it to you" (John 16:13-14).

Some define it as "a living word from the written Word". It is a word given for a specific time and purpose. It may even be a theme.

11. Part of the body sensitised

The word of knowledge may come in the form of a tingling, warm sensation, or sharp pain. Our body must be yielded to the Holy Spirit to receive such words of knowledge.

12. Dream

"Now Joseph dreamed a dream...Then he dreamed still another dream and told it to his brothers..." *(Gen 37:5-11).*

"At Gibeon the Lord appeared to Solomon in a dream by night..." (1 Kgs 3:5).

A vast majority of our dreams are from our own subconscious minds; formed by an intricate kaleidoscopic mix of data from our memory bank. "For a dream comes through much activity..." (Ecc 5:3). It is also possible to have dreams or nightmares from demonic influence and sources. Being a spirit being, it is possible to receive such dreams in our subconscious mind or spirit, from the enemy that is transmitting it. They normally sow fear, suspicion, doubt or confusion. The enemy may use bad dreams to disturb our rest. Praying in tongues just before we sleep will help to guard our subconscious mind. There are also dreams which are from the Spirit of God. We must pray to have the right interpretations to them.

"I will pour out My Spirit on all flesh...your old men shall dream dreams..." (Joel 2:28).

On several occasions, God has shown me things to come through dreams, even though I am not an old man yet.

13. Open and closed visions (Acts 9:12)

"And I, Daniel, alone saw the vision, for the men who were with me did not see the vision..." (Dan 10:7).

An open vision is seen with our natural eyes open. This is less common. A closed vision is seen with our eyes closed. The books of Daniel and Revelation are full of pictures and symbols.

14. Audible voice

"And the Holy Spirit descended in bodily form like a dove upon Him, and a voice came from heaven which said, 'You are My beloved Son; in You I am well pleased.'" (Luke 3:22).

"Then a voice came from heaven..." (John 12:28).

Even though this form of communication is less common, I personally know a number of people who have heard God speak to them audibly.

15. Angelic messenger

"Now in the sixth month the angel Gabriel was sent by God to a city of Galilee named Nazareth, to a virgin betrothed to a man whose name was Joseph, of the house of David. The virgin's name was Mary. And having come in, the angel said to her..." (Luke 1:26-38).

"And when the angel who spoke to him had departed, Cornelius called two of his household servants and a devout soldier from among those who waited on him continually" (Acts 10:7).

The Greek word for angel is *aggelos*, meaning 'messenger'.

16. The word of knowledge and wisdom (1 Cor 12:8)

The word of knowledge and wisdom is a revelation from the Holy Spirit that enables the believer to know information, facts, and the right course of action.

17. Operation of the gift of discernment (1 Cor 12:10)

The gift of discernment is not the gift of suspicion. It is the ability to distinguish and detect if the spirit is of the enemy, the self or of God.

18. Prophetic flow from within

Sometimes we may receive revelation from a spontaneous utterance while we are praying.

19. Perception and intuition

Our spirit man is capable of sensing and knowing things in another person's spirit. Jesus often perceived what was in the hearts and minds of men.

"For what man knows the things of a man except the spirit of the man which is in him? Even so no one knows the things of God except the Spirit of God" (1 Cor 2:11).

20. Prophecy

The Word of God is given when the spirit of prophecy is present. It may be given by those who have the gift of prophecy or by those who stand in the office of a prophet.

21. Holy Spirit

"the Spirit said to him..." (Acts 10:19).

22. Trance

"Then he became very hungry and wanted to eat; but while they made ready, he fell into a trance..." (Acts 10:10).

When a person is in a trance, his natural senses are in a state of suspension.

23. Circumstances

Often, God uses the circumstances of life to speak to us. For example, Paul desired to visit Rome but was unable to do it. Later, he was taken as a prisoner to Rome.

24. The Life of Christ

Jesus is the Supreme Prophet. God speaks to us through the life of Jesus – through all His words and deeds.

25. Counsel of the wise and elderly

Their accumulated knowledge and experience are valuable. Do not despise their counsel.

Since this realm is subjective in nature, it is important to:

1. Test the spirit and not be gullible to every thought or impulse we receive.

   "Beloved, do not believe every spirit, but test the spirits, whether they are of God; because many false prophets have gone out into the world" (1 John 4:1).

2. Have different sources of witness and confirmation. The witness of Scriptures, the witness of peace within and confirmations from other mature Christians or church leadership are very important and must be considered.

3. Check the "revelation" with others if it is something major.

4. Keep exercising our spiritual senses until our discernment is sharpened.

   "those who by reason of use have their senses exercised to discern both good and evil" (Heb 5:14).

Hearing from God requires time and concentration - it involves yielding to Him our total being.

Chapter 5

The Generation
With The Multiple Anointing

1. David's Threefold Anointing

2. Anointing Challenged and Tested

3. Multiple Anointings

4. Corporate Anointing

5. The Anointing Within and From Above

6. Anointing - Danger of Imitation

7. Maintaining the Anointing

8. Testimony

"The Spirit of the Lord God is upon Me,
Because the Lord has anointed Me
To preach good tidings to the poor;
He has sent Me to heal the brokenhearted,
To proclaim liberty to the captives,
And the opening of the prison to those who are bound;
To proclaim the acceptable year of the Lord,
And the day of vengeance of our God;
To comfort all who mourn,
To console those who mourn in Zion,
To give them beauty for ashes, the oil of joy for mourning,
The garment of praise for the spirit of heaviness;
That they may be called trees of righteousness,
The planting of the Lord, that He may be glorified."

(Isaiah 61:1-3)

DAVID'S THREEFOLD ANOINTING

*"Then Samuel took the horn of oil and **anointed him** in the midst of his brothers; and the Spirit of the Lord came upon David from that day forward..."* (1 Sam 16:13).

*"Then the men of Judah came, and there they **anointed David** king over the house of Judah..."* (2 Sam 2:4).

*"So all the elders of Israel came to the king at Hebron, and King David made a covenant with them at Hebron before the Lord. And they **anointed David** king over Israel"* (2 Sam 5:3).

In Old Testament days, the anointing with oil was a formal way of inducting leaders into office. We read of priests, prophets, and kings being anointed (Exo 30:30; 2 Sam 5:3; 1 Kgs 19:16). What is unique about King David is that he held three offices, that of priest, prophet, and king. David was the first and only king of Israel to be bestowed this tri-office.

There is great significance in King David's three anointings. **With each anointing upon his life, his scope of influence and level of authority increased**. I believe the anointing is the Holy Spirit's enablement and energising power. When the anointing is upon us, our spirit, soul and body function at their best. It causes us to rise above our natural capabilities. King David received his first anointing through the apostolic prophet, Samuel. Apostles and prophets have the ability to impart spiritual gifts and anointing. "For I long to see you, that I may impart to you some spiritual gift, so that you may be established..." (Rom 1:11). These are people with spiritual assets. "Silver and gold I do not have, but what I do have I give you..." (Acts 3:6).

David received his second anointing in Hebron, as king over Judah. The anointing he received in Hebron is a type of the corporate anointing. Hebron means association, league, confederacy. A strong church is one that has developed its corporate anointing, which is very powerful. Many churches depend solely upon the giftings and anointing of the minister. That is not healthy. It is like having only one strong arm, while the other members of the body have atrophied through lack of exercise. A healthy church has her members spiritually activated and mobilised for service.

A strong church is one that has developed its corporate anointing, which is very powerful.

---

*"according to the effective working by which **every part** does its share, causes growth of the body for the edifying of itself in love" (Eph 4:16).*

The third anointing David received was from the elders of Israel as king over the whole nation of Israel. It is a type of the spirit of dominion - the authority and power to rule and conquer. After receiving the third anointing, King David defeated all his foes, conquered territories, and brought the kingdom of Israel to the greatest glory in all of her history.

After receiving the third anointing, King David defeated all his foes, conquered territories, and brought the kingdom of Israel to the greatest glory in all of her history.

This present Davidic Generation is most privileged to receive and experience the multiple anointings that the Lord is giving His people in these last days. These anointings are to enable and empower yielded Christians to fulfill His divine purposes.

Smith Wigglesworth said that it is a luxury to be filled with the Holy Spirit. This blessing is the result of God's grace abounding towards us and not because we are better than past generations. Many servants of God are receiving unusual divine enpowerments. With the blessing of God's multiple anointings, we are witnessing new exploits and demonstrations of the Holy Spirit's power. As more and more of God's servants move and mature in the anointings, we can expect to see greater breakthroughs and manifestations of the power of the Holy Spirit. They will be able to do things in the spirit that they have not done before. "Most assuredly, I say to you, he who believes in Me, the works that I do he will do also; and greater works than these he will do, because I go to My Father" (John 14:12).

However, not all Christians will see such a manifestation of the multiple anointings of God in their lives even though they may be touched by it. **Since the empowerment is given to accomplish divine purposes (Isaiah 61), it will only be given and manifested in the lives of those who are continually yielded and responsive to the Holy Spirit - those whom the Holy Spirit can move upon consistently.** Those who refuse to serve the purposes of God and fail to respond to the Holy Spirit will become the 'unanointed' or 'ex-anointed', like King Saul.

ANOINTING CHALLENGED AND TESTED

Immediately after Jesus was filled with the Holy Spirit, He was driven by the Spirit into the wilderness where He was tested and tempted forty days by the devil. "Then Jesus, being filled with the Holy Spirit, returned from the Jordan and was led by the Spirit into the wilderness, being tempted for forty days by the devil. And in those days He ate nothing, and afterward, when they had ended, He was hungry" (Luke 4:1-2).

When the Philistines heard that David was anointed king over Israel, they immediately mobilised their forces to challenge and attack him: "Now when the Philistines heard that they had anointed David king over Israel, all the Philistines went up to search for David. And David heard of it and went down to the stronghold. The Philistines also went and deployed themselves in the valley of Rephaim" (2 Sam 5:17-18).

The anointing empowers you and makes you more effective in your service to God. It makes your spirit strong. The anointing that comes upon you has an immediate effect against demonic powers. It marks you out and also makes you a definite threat to the kingdom of darkness. That is why, when a new anointing comes upon you, the enemy will try to attack immediately, either to steal the anointing or hinder its full development in your life. Therefore, when you receive a double portion of anointing, be prepared to face 'double trouble' from the enemy!

The anointing that comes upon you has an immediate effect against demonic powers. It marks you out and also makes you a definite threat to the kingdom of darkness.

Note that demons have a limited measure of power. It takes a stronger power to overcome a lesser power. This power comes with the anointing of the Holy Spirit:

"But if I cast out demons with the finger of God, surely the kingdom of God has come upon you. When a strong man, fully armed, guards his own palace, his goods are in peace. But when a stronger than he comes upon him and overcomes him, he

takes from him all his armor in which he trusted, and divides his spoils" (Luke 11:20-22).

MULTIPLE ANOINTINGS

The multiple anointings come through:

1. The outpouring of God's Spirit in these last days

"Be glad then, you children of Zion, and rejoice in the Lord your God; for He has given you the former rain faithfully...and the latter rain in the first month" (Joel 2:23).

"And it shall come to pass afterward that I will pour out My Spirit on all flesh..." (Joel 2:28).

"I will pour out My Spirit in those days" (Joel 2:29).

Believers all over the world are receiving a measure of the anointing when they receive the infilling of the Holy Spirit in their lives.

2. Impartation

"Now Joshua the son of Nun was full of the Spirit of wisdom, for Moses had laid his hands on him..." (Deut 34:9).

"And the Lord said to Moses: 'Take Joshua the son of Nun with you, a man in whom is the Spirit, and lay your hand on him...And he laid his hands on him and inaugurated him, just as the Lord commanded by the hand of Moses" (Num 27:18, 23).

Impartation can take place through the laying on of hands, prayer and conduction in the spirit realm. Some call it spiritual transference. This impartation can come from someone who is full of the Spirit. These people carry a strong anointing in their lives. There can be weak or strong impartation. Doubt, unbelief and soul blockage may hinder the reception of the impartation. Therefore the recipient's heart and spirit must be prepared. Gifts of the Holy Spirit can be imparted through the laying on of hands, e.g. Paul and Timothy (1 Tim 4:14).

The offices of the prophet and apostle are being restored in this present move of God's Spirit. As thousands of prophets and apostles go forth to minister, the anointing that is upon them is being released. Believers are tasting and are being touched by their anointing.

3. "Rubbing" with ministries

In Hebrew, the primary verbal root word for 'anoint' is *mashach*. It means to rub with oil or to besmear. The strong and fresh anointing that another person carries can be rubbed upon us. Certain strengths and anointings developed in the spirit of a man can be imparted in a kind of spiritual cross pollination. Such an impartation can be received through the atmosphere of an anointed service, seminar, convention, or revival meeting. That is why they often say the anointing is caught rather than taught.

4. Angels

"And the angel answered and said to him, 'I am Gabriel, who stands in the presence of God...'" (Luke 1:19).

When angelic beings dwell in proximity to the throne of God, they are infused and saturated with the glory and anointing that emanate from Him (Exo 34:28-30). So, angels coming directly from God's presence carry with them a fresh and strong anointing. Often, the anointing will be stronger when there are a greater number of angels present. However, there are different types of angels. Since some angels are bigger and stronger than others, one powerful angel alone could produce a great effect on the atmosphere.

In one of the most memorable meetings we had, angels were seen standing, shoulder to shoulder, all around the meeting hall. On that day, the presence of God and His anointing saturated the atmosphere throughout the whole afternoon. There was a sense of great peace, joy, liberty, and inner reverence in our hearts. After the service, I observed that the people in the meeting hall walked about lightly and quietly. When they talked, they did so softly; being still very conscious of the presence of God in the place. This wonderful, heavenly atmosphere lingered and lasted for about six hours!

"And I saw still another mighty angel coming down from heaven, clothed with a cloud. And a rainbow was on his head, his face was like the sun, and his feet like pillars of fire" (Rev 10:1).

5. Anointing through association

The spirit of David influenced and transformed his men. Likewise, the anointing may be received through close and constant association with men and women of God, for example:

a. Moses with Joshua.
b. Elijah with Elisha.
c. Jesus with the twelve disciples.
d. Paul with Timothy.

6. Righteousness

"You love righteousness and hate wickedness; therefore God, Your God, has anointed You with the oil of gladness more than Your companions" *(Ps 45:7).*

When we walk in righteousness, God's sovereign anointing will be poured upon us. It is a sign and stamp of Divine approval.

CORPORATE ANOINTING

Corporate anointing is very powerful because it has the combined strength of various anointings. Certain apostles, prophets, evangelists, pastors, and teachers carry strong anointings in their lives. Imagine the strength and manifestation of these anointings when they are released together with the anointing of the saints! Many small tributaries joined together can form a mighty river.

In some of our church services such strong and

powerful anointing have been manifest. In one case, a sister who had been suffering from a severe migraine for three days was instantly healed and delivered the moment she stepped into the service, while the people were still worshipping. In another instance, a deaconess had to walk supported against the wall lest she fall. On yet another occasion, a brother felt God's presence in such an awesome way that he had to kneel the moment he stepped into the sanctuary. Many times, people just wept during the services. Others have testified to His wonderful cleansing and healing presence.

The combined release of the anointing, from spiritually activated Christians who dwell in love and unity, is a major key to the manifestation of this powerful corporate anointing.

The combined release of the anointing, from spiritually activated Christians who dwell in love and unity, is a major key to the manifestation of this powerful corporate anointing.

THE ANOINTING WITHIN AND FROM ABOVE

Our spirit man can receive and temporarily store anointing like a battery or capacitor. This anointing in our spirit can be built up as well as depleted. One can build up the anointing within, primarily through consistent reading of the Word of God, prayer, speaking in tongues, and waiting on the Lord.

Conversely, anointing can be depleted through 'leaks'. Leaks happen by way of backsliding, self-glorification and other sins. It can also diminish through negligence in building up oneself. The anointing can also be expended during ministry, when we pray for many individuals and during spiritual impartations.

"But Jesus said, 'Somebody touched Me, for I perceived power going out from Me'" (Luke 8:46).

Just as the small motorcycle battery's capacity to store charge differs widely from that of a tractor's big battery, a Christian's capacity to store and build up the anointing varies from person to person. Those who have grown spiritually, would have a more developed spirit. Their spirits are developed through spiritual exercises like prayer, ministering and shouldering spiritual responsibilities. Therefore, their spirits, being stronger, have a greater capacity to receive, accumulate and release the anointing.

The anointing from above, which is from God, has great power. He is like the sun that charges solar battery cells (our spirit). A battery can run out of power if it is not recharged. **In a service, when the minister's spirit is able to 'lock on' securely and link up with this anointing from above, there will be an undiminished flow of the anointing and a continuous charging of one's spirit from God.** When this happens, the anointing will be so intensified that it will be conducted through the air and will be felt in the whole meeting place or auditorium. The anointing will also be sustained for the whole duration of the service. For this to happen, intensive preparation of the individual's spirit, soul and body is needed. There must be a deep consciousness of His presence. It is important to minimise distractions in the service so that the consciousness of the anointing is not broken.

ANOINTING - DANGER OF IMITATION

"It shall not be poured...nor shall you make any other like it, according to its composition..." (Exo 30:32).

Since there are some people who fall because of the anointing, many have mistaken one for the other. It is true that together with the anointing, there is a tangible force or energy that touches an individual and may cause him/her to fall. However, there are other reasons why some people fall.

Below are some possible reasons why some people may fall other than the anointing of God:

1. Pressure to perform - due to the misconceived association of falling with the anointing, there are people who feel pressured to perform. They wrongly expect people to fall in every service. As a result, people are pushed over physically.

2. Ego problem - trying too hard to impress.

3. Deception and manipulation - sometimes it is outright deception and manipulation on the part of the minister. In such instances, the believer ought to be mature enough to distinguish between genuine anointing and fleshly performance.

4. Auto suggestion - we must be careful to speak only the things we truly sense in the spirit.

5. Lost equilibrium - some individuals lose their equilibrium due to closed eyes and raised hands for a period of time or when they stand on unlevel ground.

6. Peer pressure - concern about what others will think of them if they do not fall.

7. Psychological reaction and misconception - thinking that one will receive a blessing when one falls down and not otherwise.

8. Demonic reaction - demonic reaction to the anointing.

9. Sudden shock - the shock of a sudden shout or utterance.

10. Public embarrassment - being publicly scolded for resisting the Holy Spirit if they do not fall.

11. Any combination of the above factors.

May God deliver us from all the unrighteous manipulations briefly mentioned above. We, especially the ministers of the Gospel, have to be very honest and not try to fake the work of the Holy Spirit. In all that we say and do, we must reflect the nature and character of God and not misrepresent Him (Heb 1:3). Man looks to outward manifestations. But God looks at the heart.

There have been times when the anointing was so strongly manifested that people fell under the power when I prayed for them, even though I did not touch them. Recently, I ministered in a seminar for pastors and leaders in Myanmar. Many of them fell under the power simultaneously when the anointing was released upon them even from a distance.

"Now, as he was speaking with me, I was in a deep sleep with my face to the ground..." (Dan 8:18).

"And when I saw Him, I fell at His feet as dead..." (Rev 1:17).

There is a genuine tangible force and energy that comes with the anointing which can be felt and experienced by individuals. The anointing is Divine enablement and energy. I would liken it to a strong current that overpowers. Sometimes, when an individual falls, it is as if the system of the individual was unable to withstand the "voltage of the current". In some instances, the individual may fall when he comes into contact with the 'force field' or the power of the anointing that comes upon him. An aura of energy clothes the person who is deeply anointed. Falling is not the important thing. It is receiving the deep touch of the Holy Spirit that matters most.

MAINTAINING THE ANOINTING

Some say that it is easier to receive the anointing than to keep it. Honouring the Holy Spirit and acknowledging His Lordship are the major keys to keeping the anointing. We must protect and maintain the anointing that we have received.

Certain individuals who were once powerfully anointed but subsequently lost it due to various reasons become very vulnerable spiritually. When King Saul lost the anointing, he was vulnerable to tormenting spirits which afflicted him constantly. He started to act irrationally and became an impulsive, raging man. The raging Saul attempted to kill David repeatedly and he even almost speared his own son Jonathan. "But the Spirit of the Lord departed from Saul, and a distressing spirit from the Lord troubled him. And Saul's servants said to him, 'Surely, a distressing spirit from God is troubling you'" (1 Sam 16:14-15).

When the mighty Samson lost the anointing, he became weak and ordinary:

"then I shall become weak, and be like any other man" *(Jdg 16:7).*

"then I shall become weak, and be like any other man" *(Jdg 16:11).*

"and I shall become weak, and be like any other man" *(Jdg 16:17).*

When Samson finally became weak like any other man, the Philistines were able to capture him. They gouged out his eyes and made him a grinder in the prison. They humiliated him by making him a public clown.

"And she said, 'The Philistines are upon you, Samson!' So he awoke from his sleep, and said, 'I will go out as before, at other times, and shake myself free!' But he did not know that the Lord had departed from him. Then the Philistines took him and put out his eyes, and brought him down to Gaza. They bound him with bronze fetters, and he became a grinder in the prison" (Jdg 16:20-21).

Do not lose your anointing. Do not let the enemy make you weak like any other man. When a leader loses the anointing, he loses spiritual authority and power as well. Such a person may resort to substituting true spiritual authority and power with ecclesiastical control and human manipulation. In other words, politicking! In his insecurity, he will tend to implement more rules and laws to augment his position. When there are more and more rules and laws, there is less love and grace.

Honouring the Holy Spirit and acknowledging His Lordship are two of the most important keys to maintaining the anointing in your life.

Honouring the Holy Spirit and acknowledging His Lordship are two of the most important keys to maintaining the anointing in your life.

TESTIMONY

"The Spirit of the Lord God is upon Me, because the Lord has anointed Me..." (Isa 61:1).

The first time I experienced a very powerful anointing of the Lord was in 1975. I was scheduled to preach to the Christian students' fellowship for the visually handicapped at Setapak, Kuala Lumpur. They were called Young Crusaders for Christ. I was then just a few years old in the Lord.

The night before the preaching engagement, I prayed and sought the Lord earnestly. At around midnight, a powerful anointing of the Holy Spirit suddenly descended upon me. I felt a band of intense, vibrating current around my head. This band of current began to move downwards slowly, from my head to my waist and then it gradually began to surge back up to the crown of my head. This was repeated twice before it lifted.

Though I did not know much about the anointing at that time, I knew something unusual and wonderful had happened. My spirit was so quickened that I could not fall asleep until the early hours of the morning. I woke up a few hours later and went for the scheduled meeting. What happened there really surprised me.

"While Peter was still speaking these words, the Holy Spirit fell upon all those who heard the word" (Acts 10:44).

That Saturday morning I preached on the baptism of

the Holy Spirit with an unusual confidence to approximately 20 students who were seated in a circle. At the end of the message, I prayed for them to receive the baptism. However, before I could finish praying, the Holy Spirit fell upon them simultaneously! They were weeping, praying aloud in tongues and some fell down on the floor of the classroom. I had not anticipated such a quick response. So, when all this happened, I was caught by surprise and panicked a little. After regaining my composure, I tried to calm some of them who were weeping and praying in tongues loudly. I also tried to get those who had fallen on the floor seated again. My efforts were futile. They were so filled with the Spirit that they were oblivious to all else. At that time, I was afraid that the loud 'commotion' might draw unwanted attention from the school authorities. I really did not know what to do, so I just let them pray on. Later, as I left the school, I praised God for baptising the students in such a sovereign manner.

It was several days later that I received a more comprehensive report from some of the students, concerning what had actually transpired that morning and the events thereafter. All of the students were filled with the Holy Spirit and spoke in tongues except for one. Some of them saw tongues of fire over one another's heads. One of them even tried to touch the flame. A few of them had their sight momentarily restored (remember, these were students from the school for the visually handicapped). Some saw for the first time the beautiful colours of their clothing. Others heard heavenly music and singing. After that experience, the Christians continued in the spirit of revival for the next few days, praying and seeking the Lord. Why they were not permanently healed, I do not know and cannot explain.

Soon after this exciting experience, I felt led to pioneer a church, Siloam Assembly of God, in the vicinity of this school in Setapak. That was in late 1976. The signs and wonders that happened were like a divine confirmation that God was leading me to the north-eastern part of Kuala Lumpur. Through this pioneering work, another eight churches were planted within the next ten years. Today, many of them are progressing well and a few have even outgrown the mother church!

"And they went out and preached everywhere, the Lord working with them and confirming the word through the accompanying signs. Amen" (Mark 16:20).

"God also bearing witness both with signs and wonders, with various miracles, and gifts of the Holy Spirit, according to His own will?" (Heb 2:4).

Chapter 6

The Generation That Ushers Back The Ark Of God

1. David and the Ark of God

2. The Proper Order

3. Feast of Tabernacles

DAVID AND THE ARK OF GOD

Read 2 Samuel 6.

*"David was afraid of the Lord that day; and he said, 'How can the **ark of the Lord** come to me?'" (2 Sam 6:9).*

*"And it was told King David, saying, 'The Lord has blessed the house of Obed-Edom and all that belongs to him, because of the **ark of God.**' So David went and brought up the **ark of God** from the house of Obed-Edom to the City of David with gladness. And so it was, when those bearing the **ark of the Lord** had gone six paces, that he sacrificed oxen and fatted sheep. Then David danced before the Lord with all his might; and David was wearing a linen ephod. So David and all the house of Israel brought up the **ark of the Lord** with shouting and with the sound of the trumpet" (2 Sam 6:12-15).*

There is an important progression with spiritual significance in 2 Samuel, from chapters 6 to 8:

2 Sam 6 - David ushers the Ark into the City of David.

2 Sam 7 - David receives the Covenant from God.

2 Sam 8 - David's further conquests and dominion.

As soon as David was established king over all of Israel, he made it a top priority to usher the Ark of God back to Jerusalem. However, the first attempt to usher the Ark into the City of David, using a cart for transport, was discontinued when Uzzah was struck dead. They had failed to move the Ark of God in the proper order as prescribed in Numbers 4:5, 6, 15 and 7:9. Meanwhile, the Ark of God was brought into the house of Obed-Edom. While the Ark of God was there, his whole house and all that he had were richly blessed by the Lord:

"The ark of God remained with the family of Obed-Edom in his house three months. And the Lord blessed the house of Obed-Edom and all that he had" (1 Chron 13:14).

"And it was told King David, saying, 'The Lord has blessed the house of Obed-Edom and all that belongs to him, because of the ark of God...'" (2 Sam 6:12).

King David knew the importance of the Ark of God. To have the Ark close to him in Jerusalem meant having the blessing, protection, and presence of God.

King David knew the importance of the Ark of God. To have the Ark close to him in Jerusalem meant having the blessing, protection, and presence of God. The Ark is symbolic of God's throne upon the earth. It speaks of the presence and power of God. Just as the presence of God prospered Obed-Edom and all that belonged to him, likewise the presence of God can prosper our spirit, soul, and body. The power of the Ark of God was revealed in the drying up of the Jordan river (Jos 3:17) and the destruction of Dagon (1 Sam 5:1-5). It brought great destruction and judgment on the camp of the enemies:

*"Therefore they sent and gathered to themselves all the lords of the Philistines, and said, 'What shall we do with the ark of the God of Israel?' And they answered, 'Let the ark of the God of Israel be carried away to Gath.' So they carried the ark of the God of Israel away. And so it was, after they had carried it away, that the hand of the Lord was against the city with **a very great destruction**; and He struck the men of the city, both small and great, and tumors broke out on them. Therefore they sent the ark of God to Ekron. So it was, as the ark of God came to Ekron, that the Ekronites cried out, saying, 'They have brought the ark of the God of Israel to us, to kill us and our people!' So they sent and gathered together all the lords of the Philistines, and said, 'Send away the ark of the God of Israel, and let it go back to its own place, so that it does not kill us and our people.' For there was **a deadly destruction** throughout all the city; the hand of God was very heavy there. And the men who did not die were stricken with the tumors, and the cry of the city went up to heaven" (1 Sam 5:8-12).*

Later, King David made another concerted effort to bring back the Ark of God to Jerusalem. It was successful the second time, because they did it in the proper order - the Divine order.

For this special occasion, King David wore a robe of fine linen and also a linen ephod (which speaks of the priestly office) in place of his royal robe. He played music and danced with great jubilation before the Lord. The Ark was finally set in the midst of the tabernacle which King David had prepared.

The Ark speaks of the Lord Jesus Christ. Just as King David ushered back the Ark of God, this Davidic Generation will also usher the return of the Lord Jesus Christ!

Just as King David ushered back the Ark of God, this Davidic Generation will also usher the return of the Lord Jesus Christ!

THE PROPER ORDER

*"For because you did not do it the first time, the Lord our God broke out against us, because we did not consult Him about the **proper order**" (1 Chron 15:13).*

King David realised that there are God-ordained ways, the proper order, to bring the Ark of God to Jerusalem (1 Chron 15:14-28). His son, King Solomon, also observed this proper order when he brought the Ark from the Tabernacle of David to the Temple of Solomon upon its completion (2 Chron 5).

The Ark of God represented God's throne on earth in the Old Testament. In this present time, God dwells in us by His Spirit. However, for His presence to be brought into and manifested in our congregational and individual lives, this proper order must also be observed by every individual:

1. **Top Priority.** King David gave the Ark of God top priority. He perceived that to have the Ark of God with him was of utmost importance. He treasured the presence of God more than anything else. Consequently, he did not take the ushering back of the Ark to Jerusalem lightly. The elders of Israel, the military commanders, the sanctified Levites and thousands of people were assembled for the grand and joyful procession of the Ark to Jerusalem. It involved a major concerted effort (1 Chron 15:25; 2 Chron 5:2; 2 Sam 6:13-19). It was a national affair. This speaks to us that God must be first in our lives as it was in David's. "You shall have no other gods before Me" (Exo 20:3).

2. **Sanctification.** The Ark of God was brought up by sanctified priests (1 Chron 15:14; 2 Chron 5:11). The laver in the Tabernacle of Moses speaks of washing and cleansing. Before anyone can enter into the Holy Place, the person must first be cleansed. We must never take the presence of God lightly. If we want His presence to abide with us, there must be repentance and cleansing. Without sanctification and holiness, there will never be any strong manifestation of His presence and glory. "Who may ascend into the hill of the Lord? Or who may stand in His holy place? He who has clean hands and a pure heart..." (Ps 24:3-4). Jesus sanctified Himself for

our sakes and we, who desire to serve Him, should do likewise (John 17:19).

3. **Consecration.** The Levites carried the Ark of God upon their shoulders (1 Chron 15:15). This speaks of carrying the presence of God in our lives. It involves personal responsibility, which the shoulders represent. We cannot depend on others or rely on the 'worldly cart' to do it on our behalf. No machinery or electronic gadgets can ever substitute seeking Him face to face.

There may be times when we enjoy the overflow of His presence that others in the congregation carry. But the moment we are alone, it is our own spiritual discipline that will see us through and enable us to draw down His presence upon our own lives. There is no substitute for personal consecration.

4. **Praise and Worship.** The procession of the Ark was accompanied by the singing of the Levites and the joyful sound of many musical instruments. The singers raised their voice with resounding joy while others danced before the Lord in great jubilation (1 Chron 15:16).

Praise prepares and paves the way for the King of glory to come in. When we praise the Lord, we also impose silence on the enemy (Ps 8:2)! Worship is the highest and noblest activity of the human spirit. It is both an expression of our love and reverence to the Lord, as well as our response to the revelation of Himself. When we worship in the spirit, we draw near to Him and He draws close to us. If we want to usher the Ark (presence of God) into our lives, praise and worship must be a very important part of our lifestyles.

5. **Sacrifices.** When the Levites ushered the Ark of God to Zion, they offered much sacrifices to the Lord (1 Chron 15:26). There are many who desire to have the deep presence of God in their lives but are unwilling to pay the price of seeking Him. They are unwilling to sacrifice.

Only those who have learned to sacrifice to and for the Lord will enjoy a deep intimacy with Him. The willingness to sacrifice reveals the depth of one's love. Jesus loved the Church and sacrificed Himself for her. When we truly love the Lord, we will be sacrificial too.

Abraham pleased God because he was prepared to sacrifice even Isaac, the son whom he loved dearly. King Solomon received favour and revelation from God after he sacrificed sheep and oxen that could not be "counted or numbered for multitude" (2 Chron 5:6). Is there an altar of sacrifice in your life?

FEAST OF TABERNACLES (Leviticus 23)

There are three major Feasts of the Lord mentioned in the Bible. All these Feasts are prophetic; they point us to Jesus Christ, the Ark of God. The first two, the Feast of Passover and the Feast of

Pentecost, have been historically and prophetically fulfilled.

The Feast of Passover - The Feast of Passover is celebrated in the first month (Nisan) of the Jewish sacred calendar. It is also called the Feast of Unleavened Bread. This Feast was fulfilled when Jesus laid down His life as the Passover Lamb at Calvary.

"Behold! The Lamb of God who takes away the sin of the world!" (John 1:29).

"For indeed Christ, our Passover, was sacrificed for us" (1 Cor 5:7).

The Feast of Pentecost - The Feast of Pentecost, also called the Feast of Weeks, is celebrated in the third month (Sivan). It was fulfilled when the Holy Spirit came on the Day of Pentecost and baptised the disciples who were gathered for prayer in the upper room.

"Now when the Day of Pentecost had fully come...And they were all filled with the Holy Spirit and began to speak with other tongues, as the Spirit gave them utterance" (Acts 2:1-4).

The Feast of Tabernacles - The Feast of Tabernacles is the last and most important feast. It is the Feast of all feasts. It is celebrated in the seventh month (Ethanim). It is a Feast to be kept forever. This Feast is also called the Feast of His Appearing. Jesus, the Ark of God, is returning soon! The prophetic fulfillment of all that the Feast of Tabernacles represents, is now!

"It shall be a statute forever in your generations. You shall celebrate it in the seventh month" (Lev 23:41).

"shall go up from year to year to worship the King...and to keep the Feast of Tabernacles" (Zech 14:16).

The prophetic fulfillment of all that the Feast of Tabernacles represents, is now!

The Feast of Tabernacles consists of three parts:
a. The Feast of Trumpets (Lev 23:23-25).
b. The Day of Atonement (*Yom Kippor*, Lev 23:26-32).
c. The Feast of Tabernacles proper (Lev 23:33-44).

The Feast of Trumpets - We are witnessing the fulfillment of the Feast of Trumpets right before our eyes. The trumpets (prophetic voice) have begun to sound all over the world. Thousands of prophets, prophetic ministries and prophetic people have risen on an unprecedented scale. We are witnessing the restoration of the prophets and prophetic ministries. These prophets are heralding the end-time move of the Spirit of God. They are calling the people's attention to what God is doing in this present time.

As they preach, prophesy, and proclaim, they are preparing the way for the mighty manifestation of the glory of God. Just as John the Baptist was sent to prepare the way for the manifestation of the Messiah,

"'The glory of this latter temple shall be greater than the former,' says the Lord of hosts..." (Hag 2:9).

The ministries of these prophets will have a purifying and cleansing effect on the Bride of Christ, exhorting the Church not to settle for anything less than what is promised in God's Word. They will inspire the Bride to reach for the utmost in God.

Their ministries will call the people to deep repentance and cleansing. It will lead to the 'Day of Atonement' in the Church of Jesus. In the Old Testament, the Day of Atonement was the only day in the whole year when the High Priest could enter into the Holy of Holies, with blood, to make atonement for the whole nation. Repentance, humility and cleansing must take place before the Church can enter fully into the Feast of Tabernacles proper. Until the Church comes to the place of purity and humility, she will not experience the mighty manifesfestation of God's power and glory.

Repentance, humility and cleansing must take place before the Church can enter fully into the Feast of Tabernacles proper.

A new season is here! The Church of the Lord Jesus Christ has entered into the final and most important time frame of God's prophetic clock for the world. From the Holy Place, the Church is being led into the Holy of Holies. Together with this new phase of development are new anointings, new revelations, new 'sounds' of worship and new manifestations of the Spirit. All believers are to experience the three Feasts in their lives - salvation (The Feast of Passover), baptism with the Holy Spirit (The Feast of Pentecost) and fullness (The Feast of Tabernacles).

A new season is here! The Church of the Lord Jesus Christ has entered into the final and most important time frame of God's prophetic clock for the world. From the Holy Place, the Church is being led into the Holy of Holies.

The Feast of Tabernacles speaks of:
1. The greatest outpouring of the Holy Spirit.
2. The greatest sacrifice.
3. The greatest ingathering.
4. The greatest manifestation of God's power and glory.
5. The time of greatest rejoicing and dance.
6. The Church moving from the Holy Place into the Holy of Holies.
7. The glorious return of the Lord Jesus for His Bride.

WEST

HOLY OF HOLIES

FEAST OF TABERNACLES

Father
Fullness
Communion
Life
Spirit

SOUTH

HOLY PLACE

FEAST OF PENTECOST

Holy Spirit
Baptism
Consecration
Truth
Soul

NORTH

OUTER COURT

FEAST OF PASSOVER

Jesus
Salvation
Cleansing
Way
Body

EAST

● ● ● ● ●

THE TABERNACLE

1. The Greatest Outpouring of the Holy Spirit

"Be glad then, you children of Zion, and rejoice in the Lord your God; for He has given you the former rain faithfully, and He will cause the rain to come down for you—the former rain, and the latter rain in the first month" (Joel 2:23).

The Feast of Tabernacles is celebrated in the month of *Ethanim,* also called *Tishri.* It is a time of perennial rain.

Ethanim - perennial (recurring rain)
Tishri - flowing brooks

Rain in the Scriptures is symbolic of:

a. The Holy Spirit

Whenever the Holy Spirit was poured out upon the people, two main things happened: **Deliverers arose and the prophetic word of the Lord was heard.**

"The Spirit of the Lord God is upon Me...to proclaim liberty to the captives, and the opening of the prison to those who are bound..." (Isa 61:1).

"But the Spirit of the Lord came upon Gideon; then he blew the trumpet, and the Abiezrites gathered behind him" (Jdg 6:34).

"Then the Spirit of the Lord came upon Jephthah, and he passed through Gilead and Manasseh, and passed through Mizpah of Gilead; and from

Mizpah of Gilead he advanced toward the people of Ammon" (Jdg 11:29).

"I will pour out My Spirit on all flesh; your sons and your daughters shall prophesy..." (Joel 2:28).

"and it happened, when the Spirit rested upon them, that they prophesied..." (Num 11:25).

"Now his father Zacharias was filled with the Holy Spirit, and prophesied, saying..." (Luke 1:67).

In this present outpouring, 'deliverers' are arising once again and the prophetic word is being heard.

b. Blessing - Leviticus 26:4; Zechariah 10:1

"For the earth which drinks in the rain that often comes upon it, and bears herbs useful for those by whom it is cultivated, receives blessing from God" (Heb 6:7).

"The Lord will open to you His good treasure, the heavens, to give the rain to your land in its season, and to bless all the work of your hand" (Deut 28:12).

c. Visitation - Psalm 65:9-10

"He will come to us like the rain, like the latter and former rain to the earth" (Hos 6:3).

"He shall come down like rain upon the mown grass, like showers that water the earth" (Ps 72:6).

d. Refreshing

"You, O God, sent a plentiful rain, whereby You confirmed Your inheritance, when it was weary" *(Ps 68:9).*

e. Word of God

"For as the rain comes down, and the snow from heaven, and do not return there, but water the earth, and make it bring forth and bud, that it may give seed to the sower and bread to the eater, so shall My word be that goes forth from My mouth; it shall not return to Me void, but it shall accomplish what I please, and it shall prosper in the thing for which I sent it" *(Isa 55:10-11).*

This outpouring is affecting every denomination worldwide. The Anglicans, Catholics, Orthodox, Methodists, Presbyterians, Lutherans and others are being filled with the Holy Spirit.

2. The Greatest Sacrifice (Numbers 28 and 29)

Sacrifices and offerings were presented to the Lord during the Feast of Passover and the Feast of Pentecost. However, the greatest amount of offerings and sacrifices were made during the Feast of Tabernacles. To experience the full blessings of the Feast of Tabernacles, we must be willing to sacrifice for the Lord. In these last days, there will be a new willingness from the people of God to give of their substance and lives unto the Lord. "Your people shall be volunteers in the day of Your power..." (Ps 110:3).

"and they spoke to Moses, saying, 'The people bring much more than enough for the service of the work which the Lord commanded us to do.' So Moses gave a commandment, and they caused it to be proclaimed throughout the camp, saying, 'Let neither man nor woman do any more work for the offering of the sanctuary.' And the people were restrained from bringing, for the material they had was sufficient for all the work to be done—indeed too much" (Exo 36:5-7).

"Nor was there anyone among them who lacked; for all who were possessors of lands or houses sold them, and brought the proceeds of the things that were sold, and laid them at the apostles' feet; and they distributed to each as anyone had need" (Acts 4:34-35).

3. The Greatest Ingathering

"Also on the fifteenth day of the seventh month, when you have gathered in the fruit of the land, you shall keep the feast of the Lord for seven days..." (Lev 23:39).

It is a time of the wine, oil and fruit harvest, the final harvest of the year. Wine speaks of joy, olive oil speaks of the anointing of the Holy Spirit and the fruit speaks of souls. It speaks of the joy and fresh anointing of the Holy Spirit and the greatest ingathering of souls into the Kingdom of God. The nets of the churches must be mended and the folds prepared. When the Lord of the harvest releases the harvest to us, we must be ready and not lose it!

"Therefore pray the Lord of the harvest to send out laborers into His harvest" (Matt 9:38).

4. The Greatest Manifestation of God's Power and Glory

*"'and I will shake all nations, and they shall come to the Desire of All Nations, and **I will fill this temple with glory**,' says the Lord of hosts. 'The silver is Mine, and the gold is Mine,' says the Lord of hosts. '**The glory of this latter temple shall be greater than the former**,' says the Lord of hosts. 'And in this place I will give peace,' says the Lord of hosts" (Hag 2:7-9).*

This prophecy by Haggai was given during the Feast of Tabernacles. The Ark of God was also taken from Mount Zion and placed in the Temple of Solomon during the Feast of Tabernacles. "And all the men of Israel assembled to King Solomon at the feast in the month of Ethanim, which is the seventh month. Then all the elders of Israel came, and the priests took up the ark" (1 Kgs 8:2-3).

We will see a mighty, sovereign move and manifestation of God in the coming days. When the glory of God was manifest in the Temple of Solomon, even the priests had to withdraw from ministering. Like the priests, we will move out of God's way and behold His glory. **This glory of God will be manifest, particularly in His house (congregations, churches and individual lives) that has become His true temple**.

5. The Time of Greatest Rejoicing and Dance

"And you shall take for yourselves on the first day the fruit of beautiful trees, branches of palm trees, the boughs of leafy trees, and willows of the brook; and you shall rejoice before the Lord your God for seven days" (Lev 23:40).

Indeed, the best and most exciting time is just before us. There will be great joy in the house of God. We shall hear the sound of joyful shouting in the house of God. There will be great joy in the Holy Spirit for all the great things that God is doing and is about to do in this end-time. The people of God will rejoice in the dance with great jubilation. The joy of the Lord is our strength and motivation.

6. The Church Moving from the Holy Place into the Holy of Holies

The Israelites were to celebrate this Feast dwelling in booths. This was to remind them to be ready to move on with the Lord. The Church is to move on with the Lord into His fullness.

*"to know the love of Christ which passes knowledge; that you may be filled with **all the fullness** of God" (Eph 3:19).*

*"For it pleased the Father that in Him **all the fullness** should dwell...For in Him dwells **all the fullness** of the Godhead bodily" (Col 1:19; 2:9).*

The Church is not just moving from glory to glory. **She is moving from the glory of the Holy**

Place into the most glorious of all, the Holy of Holies. This is the place of glory, revelation and fullness. When we move into the realm of the Holy of Holies, we will be moving from faith to faith, strength to strength, victory to victory, and breakthrough upon breakthrough.

7. The Glorious Return of the Lord Jesus for His Bride

The Feast of Tabernacles is the last of all the Feasts. It is held in the seventh month which is also the last month of the Jewish sacred calendar. Seven is the number of completion. It speaks of the end. Listed below are some recent and major signs of the return of Christ:

a. **The 'Aliyahs'** - immigration of the Jews from around the world back to Israel, particularly the mass immigration from the former Soviet Union:

   "Behold, I will bring them from the north country, and gather them from the ends of the earth..." (Jer 31:8).

b. **The restoration of apostles and prophets.** These ministries will help to prepare the Bride for Jesus.

   "Behold, I will send you Elijah the prophet before the coming of the great and dreadful day of the Lord" (Mal 4:5).

c. **The movement and emphasis towards**

internationalisation of missions - Missions activities are being accelerated.

"And this gospel of the kingdom will be preached in all the world as a witness to all the nations, and then the end will come" (Matt 24:14).

d. **The building of massive and multiple dams across the Euphrates river in Turkey which can be used to stop the flow of the river.**

"Then the sixth angel poured out his bowl on the great river Euphrates, and its water was dried up, so that the way of the kings from the east might be prepared" (Rev 16:12).

e. **The unifying of the European Community.**

"Thus he said: 'The fourth beast shall be a fourth kingdom on earth, which shall be different from all other kingdoms, and shall devour the whole earth, trample it and break it in pieces. The ten horns are ten kings who shall arise from this kingdom. And another shall rise after them; he shall be different from the first ones, and shall subdue three kings. He shall speak pompous words against the Most High...and shall intend to change times and law. Then the saints shall be given into his hand for a time and times and half a time'" (Dan 7:23-25).

f. **Mounting world opinion and pressure against Israel.** This is the only nation that God still has a covenant with (Gen 15:18-21; 17:1-7; 22:15-18).

Chapter 7

The Covenant
Relationship Generation

1. Covenant Relationship - Covenant Blessings

2. Different Kinds of Relationship

3. Knowing Through Covenant Relationship

4. Judas' Failure

5. Strength Through Covenant Relationship

6. Rest in Covenant Relationship

7. Fruitfulness Through Covenant Relationship

8. For David's Sake

THE DAVIDIC COVENANT

I have found My servant David;
With My holy oil I have anointed him,
With whom My hand shall be established;
Also My arm shall strengthen him.
The enemy shall not outwit him,
Nor the son of wickedness afflict him.
I will beat down his foes before his face,
And plague those who hate him.
But My faithfulness and My mercy shall
be with him,
And in My name his horn shall be exalted.
Also I will set his hand over the sea,
And his right hand over the rivers.
He shall cry to Me, 'You are my Father,
My God, and the rock of my salvation.'
Also I will make him My firstborn,
The highest of the kings of the earth.
My mercy I will keep for him forever,
And My covenant shall stand firm with him.
His seed also I will make to endure forever,
And his throne as the days of heaven.

Psalm 89:20-29

COVENANT RELATIONSHIP - COVENANT BLESSINGS

Read 2 Samuel 7.

*"I have made a **covenant** with My chosen, I have sworn to My servant David" (Ps 89:3).*

*"Yet He has made with me an **everlasting covenant,** ordered in all things and secure. For this is all my salvation and all my desire..." (2 Sam 23:5).*

*"Therefore know that the Lord your God, He is God, the faithful God who **keeps covenant**..." (Deut 7:9).*

Only a handful of godly people in the Old Testament had the privilege and high honour of having God make a personal covenant with them. David loved God intensely. He was a man after God's own heart. God was so pleased with David that He made an everlasting covenant with him - now referred to as **the Davidic Covenant**. "Thus says the Lord: 'If you can break My covenant with the day and My covenant with the night, so that there will not be day and night in their season, then My covenant may also be broken with David My servant, so that he shall not have a son to reign on his throne, and with the Levites, the priests, My ministers. As the host of heaven cannot be numbered, nor the sand of the sea measured, so will I multiply the descendants of David My servant and the Levites who minister to Me" (Jer 33:20-22). It is a covenant of divine blessings and promises. In other words, God initiated and committed Himself to bless David forever and ever! What a powerful assurance David received!

"And your house and your kingdom shall be established forever before you. Your throne shall be established forever" (2 Sam 7:16).

When God chooses to commit Himself to bless you, you will surely be blessed! David's covenant relationship with God is the seventh major prophetic lesson that I would like to touch on in this chapter.

David's key to receiving the covenant blessings and promises from God was his covenant relationship with God. Through the years, David cultivated a deep, strong, and personal relationship with God. This wonderful relationship influenced every aspect of David's life and accounted for the many blessings and successes he enjoyed. If we want to receive the full blessing and promises in God's Word, we must walk in covenant relationship with Him.

If we want to receive the full blessing and promises in God's Word, we must walk in covenant relationship with Him.

DIFFERENT KINDS OF RELATIONSHIP

There are many different kinds of relationships in this world. There are the casual, superficial, temporal, distant, official, and business relationship. However, a covenant relationship is different from all of these. It is a relationship of total commitment, of unfailing loyalty and depth - a lasting bond.

God desires every believer to have a personal, growing, intimate, consistent, and lasting relationship with Him—a relationship that places Him above self and above all else. It is the depth and continual growth of such a relationship that distinguishes Christians from one another. The depth of their relationship with God is the main determining factor to their effectiveness as Christian witnesses.

The true Davidic Generation is a generation consisting of Christians who have a genuine, personal, strong, and intimate relationship with the Father, Son, and Holy Spirit.

Walking in covenant relationship with God is crucial to a person's spiritual survival and fruitfulness in these last days.

The true Davidic Generation is a generation consisting of Christians who have a genuine, personal, strong, and intimate relationship with the Father, Son, and Holy Spirit.

KNOWING THROUGH COVENANT RELATIONSHIP

"Then God said, 'Let Us make man in Our image, according to Our likeness...'" (Gen 1:26).

We are made in God's image and likeness. That is the major difference between human beings and all creatures. The key to knowing our true identity and life's destiny is to know more of God, in whose image we are made. For example, when Isaiah had a revelation of the Lord (Isa 6:1-8), he came to a new and instant realisation of his own condition. Also through that encounter and revelation of the Lord, Isaiah responded to God's call and destiny for his life. A right response to God's revelation will produce marvellous changes in our lives. God has a wonderful purpose and destiny for each of us, "...as it is written: Eye has not seen, nor ear heard, nor have entered into the heart of man the things which God has prepared for those who love Him" (1 Cor 2:9).

*"The ox **knows** its owner and the donkey its master's crib; but Israel does not **know**, My people do not consider" (Isa 1:3).*

*"that I may **know** Him and the power of His resurrection, and the fellowship of His sufferings, being conformed to His death" (Phil 3:10).*

The word '**know**' (ginosko in Greek) speaks of knowing God experientially and personally. Revelational knowledge flows through the relationship we have with Him. The depth of one's revelational knowledge is determined by the intimacy one has with Him. In knowing God deeper, we will also be more able to discern His will, ways, and purposes in the diverse and often confusing situations of life. The secret things of God are revealed to those who walk in covenant relationship with Him:

"The secret of the Lord is with those who fear Him, and He will show them His covenant" (Ps 25:14).

God communicates with us within this kind of relationship. If we want to walk with revelational knowledge and insight, we must know Him and walk in covenant relationship with Him. Those who fail to do so can easily fall into deception.

The depth of one's revelational knowledge is determined by the intimacy one has with Him.

"the great dragon was cast out, that serpent of old, called the Devil and Satan, who deceives the whole world..." (Rev 12:9).

JUDAS' FAILURE

Judas' failure was tragic and detestable. For approximately three and a half years, he walked, ate, stayed, and talked with the Master, yet he never developed a personal relationship with Him. Judas had the enviable privilege of receiving the most profound teachings, hearing the most anointed sermons, and witnessing some of the most powerful miracles of Jesus. He also saw the deep compassion of Jesus and His many magnanimous acts. He was with Jesus! Yet, through it all, he remained a spectator. Judas' unwillingness and neglect in building a sincere relationship with Jesus was his fatal failure.

Judas had no sincere desire to relate to Jesus. He merely took advantage of his association with Him for personal gain. He stole from the money bag. When the time came for his relationship with Jesus to be tested (as all relationships with Him will be tested), Judas' pretention and his weak relationship with the Lord were finally exposed - he was guilty of the heinous act of betraying the Son of God.

As seen in the case of Judas, staying with someone for a long time is no guarantee that a relationship will develop. **Similarly, a person may attend church services for years, hear hundreds of sermon, tithe faithfully and yet miss the most crucial matter - developing a personal relationship with the Lord**. It is sad that there are many such people. When faced with pressures, tests, and temptations, they succumb easily. They do not have the special strength and conviction that come from personal and constant communion with God. Each of us must give priority to developing and establishing a personal relationship with the Lord, lest we fail the tests and temptations that come our way and end up like Judas.

Building a personal and growing relationship with God is most important. It is pivotal to our living and relating to all other people and things in our lives. A strong and personal relationship is based upon loyal commitment. It grows through communication and is nurtured by love. God seeks for us to have a strong and personal relationship with Him - a covenant relationship. We ought to develop a covenant relationship with God, with our spouse and with the members of the Body of Christ.

STRENGTH THROUGH COVENANT RELATIONSHIP

In this end-time, every Christian should seek to develop a growing, deep and personal relationship with God. When you nurture this personal relationship with God, a spiritual fortitude will develop in your life.

Those who neglect to build a strong, personal relationship with God will dry up spiritually. They will find it very difficult to maintain their Christian witness in the days to come.

The pressures of the world, the influences, temptations and spiritual attacks will continue to increase. The rain, flood, fire and winds of life will test the foundation of our relationship with the Lord.

Those who neglect to build a strong, personal relationship with God will dry up spiritually.

REST IN COVENANT RELATIONSHIP

"My covenant I will not break, nor alter the word that has gone out of My lips. Once I have sworn by My holiness; I will not lie to David" (Ps 89:34,35).

The Bible is made up of two major sections, the Old and the New Covenant. God and His word are one. His words and promises are completely reliable, for He cannot lie (Num 23:19). His unchanging nature and covenant are the bases of our trust, assurance and security. Therefore, we can rest upon God's covenant. There are too many ministers today who are insecure spiritually but those who walk in covenant relationship with Him will enjoy a special rest, trust, and security in Him. They will experience a deep restfulness within.

FRUITFULNESS THROUGH COVENANT RELATIONSHIP

"Abide in Me, and I in you. As the branch cannot bear fruit of itself, unless it abides in the vine, neither can you, unless you abide in Me. I am the vine, you are the branches. **He who abides in Me, and I in him, bears much fruit**; *for without Me you can do nothing. If anyone does not abide in Me, he is cast out as a branch and is withered; and they gather them and throw them into the fire, and they are burned" (John 15:4-6).*

The Greek word for *abide* is *meno*. It means to remain, dwell, endure and last. In the passage above, it conveys two main thoughts - **intimacy** and **permanency**.

True fruitfulness in our lives is largely determined by the relationship we have with Jesus. Those who are fruitful are those who have an intimate and enduring relationship with Him. It is through such covenant relationship that His divine supply of grace, wisdom, love and power flows through us. Fruitfulness results when He indwells and overflows through our lives. Fruitfulness is a natural result when we are one with Him. Those who are far from God and those who constantly vacillate in their relationship with the Lord will not accomplish much, neither will they be fruitful.

*"For indeed, those who are **far** from You shall perish; You have destroyed all those who desert You for harlotry. But it is good for me to draw **near** to God; I have put my trust in the Lord God, that I may declare all Your works" (Ps 73:27-28).*

*"These people draw **near** to Me with their mouth, and honor Me with their lips, but their heart is **far** from Me" (Matt 15:8).*

Younger people want lots of action and instant results. They tend to be activity- or task-oriented. At times, in their quest to reach their goals, they become brusque with people.

However, those who are more mature are people-oriented. They esteem the worth of an individual. They know the value of building good relationships. This may entail a long and slow process but its benefits and blessings last a lifetime.

Fruitfulness is a natural result when we are one with Him.

FOR DAVID'S SAKE

The Hebrew word for 'sake' is *ma'an*, meaning on account of, in order that, because of, to the intent that.

The phrase **'for David's sake'** shows us that God is committed to honour His covenant with David. It also shows how much David meant to Him. Many people in the Old Testament benefitted from King David's favoured standing and covenant relationship with God. It is because of David that they enjoyed special grace, protection, and provision.

*"Nevertheless I will not do it in your days, **for the sake of your father David**; but I will tear it out of the hand of your son" (1 Kgs 11:12).*

*"However I will not tear away the whole kingdom, but I will give one tribe to your son **for the sake of my servant David**, and for the sake of Jerusalem which I have chosen" (1 Kgs 11:13).*

*"However I will not take the whole kingdom out of his hand, because I have made him ruler all the days of his life **for the sake of My servant David**, whom I chose because he kept My commandments and My statutes" (1 Kgs 11:34).*

*"Nevertheless **for David's sake** the Lord his God gave him a lamp in Jerusalem, by setting up his son after him and by establishing Jerusalem" (1 Kgs 15:4).*

*"Yet the Lord would not destroy Judah, **for the sake of his servant David**, as He promised him to give a lamp to him and his sons forever" (2 Kgs 8:19).*

*"For I will defend this city, to save it for My own sake and **for My servant David's sake**" (2 Kgs 19:34).*

*"And I will add to your days fifteen years. I will deliver you and this city from the hand of the king of Assyria; and I will defend this city for My own sake, and **for the sake of My servant David**" (2 Kgs 20:6).*

Today, many of us are benefitting from Christ's favoured standing and covenant relationship with the Heavenly Father. "Who is he who condemns? It is Christ who died, and furthermore is also risen, who is even at the right hand of God, who also makes intercession for us" (Rom 8:34). Today, for Christ's sake, we are forgiven, delivered, saved, healed and blessed. *'For the sake of Jesus'* and *'In the name of Jesus'* are powerful phrases when used in prayer. It invokes the New Covenant made by Jesus through His blood:

"Likewise He also took the cup after supper, saying, 'This cup is the new covenant in My blood, which is shed for you'" (Luke 22:20).

If God's covenant with King David resulted in much favour, grace and blessing to some in the past; then God's covenant with Christ (the Greater David) will result in even more favour, grace and blessing to us today. Christ is the Mediator of a better covenant for us today.

*"by so much more Jesus has become a surety of a **better covenant**" (Heb 7:22).*

*"But now He has obtained a more excellent ministry, inasmuch as He is also Mediator of **a better covenant**, which was established on better promises" (Heb 8:6).*

If God's covenant with King David resulted in much favour, grace and blessing to some in the past; then God's covenant with Christ (the Greater David) will result in even more favour, grace and blessing to us today.

Chapter 8

The Dominion

1. King David's Dominion

2. Character, Power and Dominion

3. Jesus, the Man of Dominion

4. Dominion Over Spirits

5. The Spirit of Dominion

6. A Memorable Service

7. Dominion Level

8. Fruits and Results of Dominion

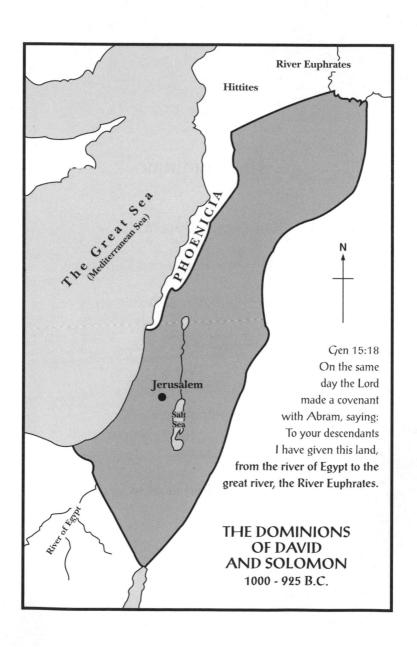

River Euphrates

Hittites

The Great Sea
(Mediterranean Sea)

PHOENICIA

N

Jerusalem

Salt
Sea

Gen 15:18
On the same
day the Lord
made a covenant
with Abram, saying:
To your descendants
I have given this land,
from the river of Egypt to the
great river, the River Euphrates.

River of Egypt

THE DOMINIONS
OF DAVID
AND SOLOMON
1000 - 925 B.C.

KING DAVID'S DOMINION

After King David received the Divine Covenant, he expanded his kingdom in all directions, conquering lands that the Joshua Generation could not possess. From 1002 B.C. to about 995 B.C., King David extended the kingdom to the north, east, south and west. His empire stretched from the river of Egypt in the south to the Euphrates river in the north-east. He knew the land he should possess and he also knew where to stop (the boundary). **It was the greatest kingdom Israel has known in all her history.**

The covenant promise given by God to Abraham regarding the possession of the land was finally fulfilled during King David's reign. The period between the promise and the fulfillment was approximately 1,100 years!

"On the same day the Lord made a covenant with Abram, saying: 'To your descendants I have given this land, from the river of Egypt to the great river, the River Euphrates'" *(Gen 15:18).*

In 2 Samuel 8:1-14, we read about how King David took dominion over all his foes:

*"After this it came to pass that David **attacked** the Philistines and **subdued** them. And David **took** Metheg Ammah from the hand of the Philistines"* *(2 Sam 8:1).*

*"Then he **defeated** Moab. **Forcing** them down to the ground, he measured them off with a line. With two lines he measured off those to be put to death,*

and with one full line those to be kept alive. So the Moabites became David's servants, and **brought tribute**" *(2 Sam 8:2).*

"David also **defeated** *Hadadezer the son of Rehob, king of Zobah, as he went to* **recover** *his territory at the River Euphrates" (2 Sam 8:3).*

"David **took** *from him one thousand chariots, seven hundred horsemen, and twenty thousand foot soldiers. Also David hamstrung all the chariot horses, except that he spared enough of them for one hundred chariots" (2 Sam 8:4).*

"When the Syrians of Damascus came to help Hadadezer king of Zobah, David killed twenty-two thousand of the Syrians" (2 Sam 8:5).

"Then David put garrisons in Syria of Damascus; and the Syrians became David's servants, and brought tribute. The Lord preserved David wherever he went" (2 Sam 8:6).

"And David **took** *the shields of gold that had belonged to the servants of Hadadezer, and brought them to Jerusalem" (2 Sam 8:7).*

"Also from Betah and from Berothai, cities of Hadadezer, King David **took** *a large amount of bronze" (2 Sam 8:8).*

When David was a boy, he was anointed by the apostolic prophet Samuel (1 Sam 16:13). He was anointed a second time as king over Judah (2 Sam 2:4). David received the third anointing from the elders of Israel (2 Sam 5:3). There is a very important spiritual progression in 2 Samuel, chapters 5 to 8:

• 2 Samuel 5 - David was anointed the third time, made king over Israel and captured the stronghold of Zion (2 Sam 5:7). The Jebusites who earlier inhabited Zion were a type of the mocking and taunting spirits of the world.

• 2 Samuel 6 - The Ark of God was brought to Jerusalem.

• 2 Samuel 7 - God's covenant with David.

• 2 Samuel 8 - David's further conquests and dominion.

CHARACTER, POWER AND DOMINION

"An inheritance gained hastily at the beginning will not be blessed at the end" (Pro 20:21).

God moulded David through a long process of trials and persecutions. Through the hard times, God was teaching David and preparing him for a position of power. And, it is usually through hard times that we learn the deeper lessons of life. In fact, many of David's beautiful psalms were written during those difficult times. David had to go through the humbling experience of living in smelly, bat-infested caves before he lived in the splendour of the palace. **The loneliness and fiery trials drove David deeper into God**. The many threats from Saul made David more dependent upon God. David was hunted and pursued like an animal by the demonised King Saul. To escape from Saul's persecution mania, he had to live as a fugitive for approximately thirteen long years. There was no other refuge he could turn to. He had to depend solely upon God for consolation, safety, direction, and help. As a result, he habitually inquired of the Lord and inclined his heart towards Him. Through it all, David waited patiently for the maturation of Heaven's plan. He was not anxious to be crowned king (how unlike many who are in the ministry today). Often those with a great destiny will go through deeper preparation from God:

"knowing that the testing of your faith produces patience. But let patience have its perfect work, that you may be perfect and complete, lacking nothing" *(James 1:3-4).*

He was not anxious to be crowned king (how unlike many who are in the ministry today).

Power, spiritual or otherwise, can either be beneficial or destructive. It depends largely upon the character of the person who exercises it. King Saul abused the power he had. As a result, many innocent lives were lost. In his murderous rage, Saul ordered the massacre of eighty-five priests and all the innocent inhabitants of Nob.

Power can be alluring. Not many people can handle power, fame, or riches well. In the Bible, we read of many evil kings. In fact, the majority of Israel's kings were bad. The evil traits in them were further magnified and compounded by the powerful position they held.

Those who have power, fame or wealth but are lacking in character are standing in 'slippery places' as the Scripture puts it (Ps 73:18). They slip and fall very easily into sin, pride and tyranny. It happened to many. King Uzziah was one of them. The early part of his reign was very good but the latter part was dismal. "So his fame spread far and wide, for he was marvelously helped till he became strong. **But when he was strong his heart was lifted up, to his destruction,** for he transgressed against the Lord his God by entering the temple of the Lord to burn incense on the altar of incense" (2 Chron 26:15-16). Only the sanctified priests were allowed to burn incense on the altar.

During a spiritual lapse in King David's life, he too fell and was guilty of power abuse, adultery, and the death of Uriah the Hittite. Therefore, let him who thinks he stands, take heed, lest he fall.

One of the finest characters in the Bible is Job. He is a model for us to follow. **He had such admirable and godly qualities that, more than once, he received the highest commendation from God:** "there is none like him on the earth, a blameless and upright man, one who fears God and shuns evil" (Job 1:8).

God loved Job and was very proud of him, but, on the other hand, satan hated Job and was rabidly jealous of him. For on earth, Job's character reminded the devil so much about God in heaven. Therefore, satan attacked Job furiously. "Yes, and all who desire to live godly in Christ Jesus will suffer persecution" (2 Tim 3:12).

These are the qualities which God valued and found in Job:

1. Job was blameless - *"Therefore, beloved, looking forward to these things, be diligent to be found by Him in peace, without spot and blameless" (2 Pet 3:14).*

2. Job was upright - *"The upright shall have dominion over..." (Ps 49:14).*

3. Job feared God - *"Fear God and keep His commandments, for this is the whole duty of man" (Ecc 12:13).*

4. Job shunned evil - *"Abstain from every form of evil" (1 Thes 5:22).*

The devil has some power but no character. Job had character but 'no power' over the devil. Jesus has both character and power. It is God's desire for us to have the character of Jesus and the power of the Holy Spirit in our lives. That's balance!

In these end-times, we will see the power of God manifested in greater dimensions through believers.

God will entrust His power to those:
1. Who are blameless.
2. Who are upright.
3. Who fear God.
4. Who shun evil.
5. Who will draw deep into His presence.
6. Whose heart is governed by love and compassion.
7. Who will give Him all the glory.
8. Who will walk humbly before Him.
9. Who will obey and believe.
10. Who are broken.

"that I may not abuse my authority in the gospel" *(1 Cor 9:18).*

JESUS, THE MAN OF DOMINION

The first Adam lost the dominion when he sinned. However, the dominion was once again restored through Jesus, who is the second Adam. When Jesus came, He manifested power and dominion over everything.

1. His dominion over demons

"For with authority and power He commands the unclean spirits, and they come out" *(Luke 4:36).*

"Having disarmed principalities and powers, He made a public spectacle of them, triumphing over them in it" *(Col 2:15).*

2. His dominion over the devil

"that at the name of Jesus every knee should bow, of those in heaven, and of those on earth, and of those under the earth, and that every tongue should confess that Jesus Christ is Lord, to the glory of God the Father" (Phil 2:10-11).

3. His dominion over diseases

"they sent out into all that surrounding region, brought to Him all who were sick, and begged Him that they might only touch the hem of His garment. And as many as touched it were made perfectly well" (Matt 14:35-36).

4. His dominion over death

"I am the resurrection and the life. He who believes in Me, though he may die, he shall live" (John 11:25).

"Then He came and touched the open coffin, and those who carried him stood still. And He said, 'Young man, I say to you, arise.' And he who was dead sat up and began to speak. And He presented him to his mother" (Luke 7:14-15).

"knowing that Christ, having been raised from the dead, dies no more. Death no longer has dominion over Him" (Rom 6:9).

5. His dominion over time and space

"'Lord, by this time there is a stench, for he has been dead four days'" (John 11:39).

"He cried out with a loud voice 'Lazarus, come forth!' And he who had died came out..." (John 11:43-44).

The healing of the centurion's servant from a great distance (Matt 8:5-13).

6. His dominion over the elements

"the water that was made wine..." (John 2:9).

"And He took the five loaves and the two fish, and looking up to heaven, He blessed and broke and gave the loaves to the disciples; and the disciples gave to the multitudes. So they all ate and were filled, and they took up twelve baskets full of the fragments that remained" (Matt 14:19-20).

7. His dominion over the forces of nature

"Then He arose and rebuked the wind and the raging of the water. And they ceased, and there was a calm...For He commands even the winds and water, and they obey Him!" (Luke 8:24-25).

8. His dominion over the laws of nature

"they saw Him walking on the sea..." (Mark 6:49).

9. His dominion over all

"All authority has been given to Me in heaven and on earth" (Matt 28:18).

"far above all principality and power and might and dominion, and every name that is named,

not only in this age but also in that which is to come" (Eph 1:21).

10. His everlasting dominion

"Then to Him was given dominion and glory and a kingdom, that all peoples, nations, and languages should serve Him. His dominion is an everlasting dominion, which shall not pass away, and His kingdom the one which shall not be destroyed" (Dan 7:14).

"The kingdoms of this world have become the kingdoms of our Lord and of His Christ, and He shall reign forever and ever!" (Rev 11:15).

The dominion was restored by the second Adam so that His Bride, the Church, can have dominion, too. God desires us to become more like Jesus, not only in character but in spiritual authority and power.

There is vast supernatural power and potential in every believer who is indwelt by the Holy Spirit. If we want to accomplish much for God, these spiritual resources must be released.

DOMINION OVER SPIRITS

"You have made him to have dominion over the works of Your hands; You have put all things under his feet..." (Ps 8:6).

Jesus defeated the devil for us. The cross of Calvary symbolises Christ's victory. However, the fierce spiritual battle rages on today. This struggle is evident in every realm of influence and power. The conflict continues unabated in the hearts and minds of individuals. It will be so until Jesus returns to reign upon the earth.

Many people do not realise that much of the resistance and opposition that we encounter in our walk with the Lord comes from demonic spirits. The enemy does not want us to prosper spiritually, emotionally and physically. Demonic attacks may come in different ways. Very often, these evil spirits make use of human beings as vessels to perpetrate and project their attacks by way of intimidation, criticism, control, fear, doubt and slander. Christians who have backslidden and no longer have a prayer life are vulnerable to being influenced and used by the enemy. Yes, it is possible for unwary Christians to be demonised. We are to guard our hearts at all times and ensure that we do not give any place to the enemy. In the Gospel, we read of how satan tried to use Peter to divert Jesus from fulfilling the purpose of God:

"Then Peter took Him aside and began to rebuke Him, saying, 'Far be it from You, Lord; this shall not happen to You!' But He turned and said to Peter, 'Get behind Me, Satan! You are an offense to Me, for you are not mindful of the things of God, but the things of men'" (Matt 16:22-23).

In the course of serving the Lord, we often come against demonic spirits that operate through people who are under their influence. These people may be sitting among the congregation! People who have a controlling, critical and doubting spirit resist the preaching of God's Word. When a minister operates in the spirit of dominion, this spiritual resistance and opposition is overcome. The spirit of dominion is an anointing that subdues and prevails against such spirits.

In dealing with people in general, we must be gentle. But, when we are confronting evil spirits, we must be bold and authoritative, like the Apostle Paul when he dealt with Elymas the sorcerer:

"But Elymas the sorcerer (for so his name is translated) withstood them, seeking to turn the proconsul away from the faith. Then Saul, who also is called Paul, filled with the Holy Spirit, looked intently at him and said, 'O full of all deceit and all fraud, you son of the devil, you enemy of all righteousness, will you not cease perverting the straight ways of the Lord? And now, indeed, the hand of the Lord is upon you, and you shall be blind, not seeing the sun for a time.' And immediately a dark mist fell on him, and he went around seeking someone to lead him by the hand" (Acts 13:8-11).

THE SPIRIT OF DOMINION

*"Then God said, 'Let Us make man in Our image, according to Our likeness; let them have **dominion over** the fish...**over** the birds...and **over** the cattle, **over** all the earth and **over** every creeping thing...' So God created man in His own image; in the image of God He created him; male and female He created them. Then God blessed them, and God said to them,*

'Be fruitful...have **dominion over** *the fish...* **over** *the birds...and* **over** *every living thing...'"* (Gen 1:26-28).

The Hebrew word for dominion is *radah*. It means to tread down, to subjugate, to subdue, to rule, to prevail against, to reign and to take possession.

The spirit of dominion is the most powerful anointing to operate through a servant of God. It is the manifestation of the kingly anointing - the authority and power to rule in the spirit realm. It is an anointing that prevails. Some call it the 'heavy anointing' for it is thick and strong. Within this level, some ministers of God may operate at different degrees. The degrees are subject to their spiritual depth in God, personal breakthroughs, faith levels, offices, the sovereign blessing of God, pre-service preparation and much prayer.

Presently, not many ministers are able to move in this anointing. However in this Davidic Generation, we will see more and more servants of God move into this level. Kathryn Kuhlman walked in the spirit of dominion and she was able to minister in it consistently.

When the spirit of dominion is manifested, the atmosphere is wondrously different. You can feel a very tangible anointing in the air!

The minister who moves in this kind of anointing may be talking gently and slowly, yet there is a forceful authority that commands the attention of the audience. When this anointing is very strong, even the thoughts and attention of the people are 'arrested' and 'prevented' from straying. Usually the eyes of the people are riveted on the minister.

When the spirit of dominion is manifested, the atmosphere is wondrously different. You can feel a very tangible anointing in the air!

At times, some may close their eyes, savouring and absorbing the deep presence of God that often accompanies the manifestation of the spirit of dominion. "...all the people hung upon His words and stuck by Him" (Luke 19:48, Amplified Bible).

It is also not uncommon to see people weep in such meetings. The Word of God that goes forth from the minister is energised and empowered. It penetrates into the innermost being. The minister speaks from his spirit directly into the spirit man of the listener:

"For indeed, as soon as the voice of your greeting sounded in my ears, the babe leaped in my womb for joy" (Luke 1:44).

"And they said to one another, 'Did not our heart burn within us while He talked with us on the road, and while He opened the Scriptures to us?'" (Luke 24:32).

When the spirit of dominion is present, people are less conscious of the passage of time. Although the service may be long, yet the people do not feel tired but rather, refreshed and strengthened. This is because when the spirit of dominion is manifest, a spiritual release and infusion of the Spirit's life and energy en masse takes place at the same time:

"It is the Spirit who gives life; the flesh profits nothing. The word that I speak to you are spirit, and they are life" (John 6:63).

To operate at this level of anointing, the spirit man of the minister must be in a state of ascendancy (that is, the state of the spirit man must be dominant, in control, having come to the fore). **Those who enter often into the realm of the 'Holy of Holies' in prayer will carry such anointing in their lives.**

When the anointing is very rich and full, the minister will feel it overflowing from his whole body. The force of this anointing radiates from his being and it is normally stronger over the frontal portion of the body.

"And the whole multitude sought to touch Him, for power went out from Him and healed them all" (Luke 6:19).

While moving in this anointing, the minister will feel strong and bold. His mind is clear and his spirit, keen. There is a sense of mastery and heightened consciousness of things that are happening in the spirit realm and in the surroundings. When one has tasted this kind of anointing, the others seem weak in comparison. The best and strongest spiritual impartation comes from those who carry this kingly anointing and manifest the spirit of dominion.

Prophet Samuel, St. Francis of Assisi, John Wesley, Sadhu Sundar Singh, Charles G. Finney, D. L. Moody, John G. Lake, Maria Woodworth Etter, Kathryn Kuhlman and Benny Hinn are some examples of those who manifest the spirit of dominion to a very high degree in their ministries. These are God's generals.

An example of the power and the effects of the spirit of dominion is found in 1 Samuel 19:18-24. In this passage, the combination of the prophetic mantle, the spirit of prophecy and the corporate anointing of Samuel and the prophets are powerfully demonstrated. King Saul and all those who were sent to arrest David were themselves 'arrested' and overwhelmed by the Spirit of God instead. This is an example of complete dominion.

"Then Saul sent messengers to take David. And when they saw the group of prophets prophesying, and Samuel standing as leader over them, the Spirit of God came upon the messengers of Saul, and they also prophesied. And when Saul was told, he sent other messengers, and they prophesied likewise. Then Saul sent messengers again the third time, and they prophesied also" (1 Sam 19:20-21).

"So he went there to Naioth in Ramah. Then the Spirit of God was upon him also, and he went on and prophesied until he came to Naioth in Ramah.

And he also stripped off his clothes and prophesied before Samuel in like manner, and lay down naked all that day and all that night. Therefore they say, 'Is Saul also among the prophets?'" (1 Sam 19:23-24).

A MEMORABLE SERVICE

Some of my most memorable services have not been the biggest or the loudest meetings. They have been those that had a powerful manifestation of God's glorious presence in which I could sense the spirit of dominion. I thank God for the many memorable services He has made possible. I would like to briefly recall one of them.

One of my favourite places of prayer is my car. It is my mobile air-conditioned prayer room. I enjoy praying most when I am driving alone with suitable strains of music playing softly in the background. It is my habit to talk to the Lord and 'tune in' to Him as I drive to the venue of my preaching engagements. Early one Sunday morning, as I was driving to a meeting, I felt the anointing of God come upon me like a warm electrifying blanket covering my head and my shoulders. I was thrilled to sense this 'thick' anointing.

I basked in the anointing and allowed it to permeate my being as I continued to worship and drive on. If we take time to be saturated with the anointing, our ministry will be vastly different. When it was time for me to speak, I began by prophesying to the congregation concerning the ministry of their church.

After that, I asked the pianist to continue playing softly as I ministered the Word. The strong presence of God was tangibly felt by all. As I spoke, I noticed that many had their eyes closed and tears were streaming down their faces.

The anointing that morning was sweet, strong and sustained. I really enjoyed His wonderful presence. At the end of the service, the people came eagerly to the altar and formed a line to receive ministry.

Full of the Spirit of God, I walked down from the pulpit, worshipping and praising Him at the same time. As I walked past the row of people, a number of them fell backwards. I had not even begun to pray for them yet! Many others fell the moment I finished prophesying over them. Visions came easily and prophecies flowed smoothly that morning. Glory to God!

At the end of the service, I turned my attention to a girl who was standing about twelve feet away. Earlier, she had been busy catching many of those who were falling under the Holy Spirit's power.

I asked if she had been prayed for and she said, "No", so I decided to pray for her from that distance. When my right hand was only half raised in her direction, she collapsed backwards. I distinctly remember feeling a tangible ball of anointing in my right palm as I raised my hand. So mighty was the Lord's anointing that morning, many fell under the power of the Holy Spirit without me touching them.

After the service in this church, I returned to my own

church. The service was still in progress. My wife, who usually sits in the front row, later told me that though she did not see me, she knew I had returned because there was a stronger anointing and a distinct change in the atmosphere the moment I entered through the church door, which is located at the back of the hall.

Later in the evening, I went to The Psalmist (a coffee house ministry run by our church). Some of the members who were also at the coffee house remarked that they could still sense the strong anointing resting upon me. That unusually strong anointing abided with me through the whole day.

"But my horn You have exalted like a wild ox; I have been anointed with fresh oil" (Ps 92:10).

DOMINION LEVEL

There are different kinds of anointing and varied levels of anointing. In the Bible, we read of the anointing on the prophet, priest and king. The dominion level is a stronger level of anointing coupled with a higher level of spiritual authority.

To minister in this dominion level, the minister must have a:
a. special (sovereign) anointing from God.
b. manifest indwelling presence of Christ.
c. covenant relationship with God.

a. Special (Sovereign) Anointing from God

Great men and women of God speak of a spiritual,

definite and life-transforming experience in their life. They all testify to a special powerful anointing, divine visitation, and baptism in the Spirit. Maria Woodworth Etters, Charles G. Finney, D.L. Moody, John G. Lake, Kathryn Kuhlman, Benny Hinn, and others have all testified to receiving a special anointing from God.

I believe certain ministers of God are accorded the privilege of having more or mightier holy angels to minister alongside them because of their spiritual position in the Lord. I believe that those who have the ability to see into the spirit realm will affirm that this is true. I also believe this privilege is afforded to any ministry or believer who is willing to press deeper into God, pay the price and develop a covenant relationship with Him.

b. Manifest Indwelling Presence of Christ

"Do you not know that you are the temple of God and that the Spirit of God dwells in you?" (1 Cor 3:16).

"Now when Solomon had finished praying, fire came down from heaven and consumed the burnt offering and the sacrifices; and the glory of the Lord filled the temple" (2 Chron 7:1).

Not many believers have the indwelling presence of God manifest in their lives in a powerful manner. There may be some reasons why this is so:

1. A weak spirit - failure to observe the basic spiritual discipline of prayer and feeding upon the Word of God.

2. Soul blockage - an unrenewed mind, idolatry, carnal obsession, the need for inner healing and hereditary bondages (Rom 12:2; Exo 20:3, 5).

3. Carnal living - living just to satisfy the natural appetite and instinct. Failure to walk in the Spirit (Gal 5:16-17).

4. Prayerlessness - failure to spend quality and quantity time communing with God.

"In Your Presence is fullness of joy; at Your right hand are pleasures forevermore" (Ps 16:11).

For the indwelling presence of God to be manifest in our lives, we must recognise, reverence and treasure His presence. It is 'something' that the world cannot produce or give. Once you recognise the presence of God drawing you, be prepared to leave other things aside so that you may respond to Him fully. Enjoy His presence. Linger long and deep in His presence. Cultivate the consciousness of His presence in your life daily. Worship Him.

c. Covenant Relationship with God

"'You shall love the Lord Your God will all your heart, with all your soul, with all your strength, and with all your mind'" (Luke 10:27).

God's best anointing and His Spirit's power are for those who truly love Him and desire to glorify His name. It is for those who love God more than anything else. Those who enter into such a relationship with Him will receive a personal covenant word from the Lord or through His prophets. They will receive divine assurance and revelations concerning their destiny.

FRUITS AND RESULTS OF DOMINION

Those who claim to be prophets and apostles must have fruits and results to show. For by their fruits we shall know them. Similarly, those who move in this level of ministry will have fruits and results to show.

To move in this dominion level is to operate at the highest level of anointing. It is to begin to rule and reign with Christ. All ministries should aspire to attain to this level. It speaks of the kingly anointing and authority to rule, prevail and decree in the realm of the Spirit.

To move in this dominion level is to operate at the highest level of anointing. It is to begin to rule and reign with Christ.

I believe as the Church of Jesus matures, more and more ministers will be promoted into this level of ministry. They will taste the powers of the age to come (Heb 6:5).

"Then the kingdom and dominion, and the greatness of the kingdoms under the whole heaven, shall be given to the people, the saints of the Most High. His kingdom is an everlasting kingdom, and all dominions shall serve and obey Him" (Dan 7:27).

Hidden Valleys
(by Kelly Willard)

In a hidden valley just over the hill
A young shepherd boy surrenders his will
As he lifts his voice in praise to his King
Only the lambs will hear and follow as he sings

In a hidden valley a faithful one leads
No one looking on, he cares for their needs
For he knows the One who tries the heart
So he is steadfast and content to do his part

In a hidden valley a leader is born
He has faced the fierce and weathered the storm
So with humble heart and love for his God
He becomes royalty with just a staff and rod

Hidden valleys produce a life song
Hidden valleys will make a heart strong
Desperation can cause you to sing
Hidden valleys turn shepherds to kings

To order David Swan's books, contact:

Tabernacle of David
1 Jalan Usahawan 5
Kawasan Perindustrian Setapak
53200 Kuala Lumpur
West Malaysia

Fax: (60)3-40229690
E-mail: todavid@tm.net.my
Website: www.todavid-worship.org

UNDERSTANDING THE SPIRITUAL SEASONS OF LIFE

To everything there is a season, a time for every purpose under heaven

There are seasons in our lives. We all go through cycles of experience and different phases of change in our lifetime. We may prefer having an eternal spring-time, but God knows that for the complete and balanced development of our character, the other seasons are indispensable. So, He uses the seasons to work out His character in us and bring us to maturity.

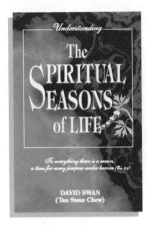

This book offers practical insights into the four spiritual seasons of life. Apart from the perils faced, it covers among other important issues, practical advice and the blessings the seasons bring. The five main sections of the book feature

- The Winter Season
- The Spring Season
- The Summer Season
- The Autumn Season
- In His Time

This book is written primarily for pastors and spiritual leaders. You have a special place in my heart.

Understanding the Spiritual Seasons of Life is amazing, I literally ate it, it gave me so much understanding about life. **– BARBARA EGELER**

This book is such an awesome accumulation of wisdom and insight into the deep things of God. I will never be the same again. Just to be able to know what God is doing and why he is doing it allows one to cooperate with the process yet see the snares before they arrive.
– MARIANNE TUCKER

MOVING INTO THE HOLY OF HOLIES

The End–Time Call of the Spirit

Indeed the Holy Spirit is drawing the Bride of Christ into the Holy of Holies, and I thank God for your book, as it has encouraged and directed me to go into deeper places in Him.

– KRIS PAGE

I must say it is a very powerful book!

– TONY PHANG

Your revelation in Moving into the Holy of Holies is absolutely awesome. I often share some of these truths in our Praise and Worship seminars and in our revival meetings. **– A. L. GILL**

The Holy Spirit at this time and hour is bidding the Bride of Christ to come into the Holy of Holies. For it is in this secret place of the Most High - the Holy of Holies, that you will receive revelations, heavenly commission and the empowerment, to do His will and fulfil your God-given destiny. This book has been translated into German and Russian.

Divided into three main sections, among the 33 topics covered include:

- Becoming One with Him
- Entering into His Rest
- Bringing Forth A Hundredfold
- The Good, the Better, and the Best
- Place of Wondrous Beauty
- The Throne Room
- The King's Table
- Where His Whispering Voice is Heard
- The Place of Transformation
- The Kingly Anointing
- Face to Face
- Clothed with His Glory

THE POWER OF PROPHETIC WORSHIP

*Releasing The Powerful Corporate Anointing
And Ushering In The Glory*

Prophetic praise and worship releases the Spirit's anointing and power in a mighty way. God is using corporate intercession, praise, worship and anointed music as His powerful end-time spiritual weapon.

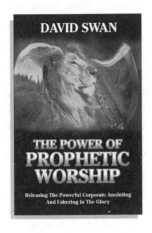

Discover the secrets of creating the open heaven, releasing angelic ministries, releasing the powerful Voice of the Lord and destroying satanic strongholds. This book has been translated into German and Russian.

Among the 43 topics covered are
- The Davids of God
- Holy Worshipping Warriors
- The Key of David
- Ushering in the Glory
- Glory Sounds
- The Power of Your Voice
- Worshipping Churches
- Anointed Music
- The Power of the Mouth
- Extravagant Worship
- Creating A Worshipful Atmosphere
- Prophets, Priests and Kings

"The Power of Prophetic Worship" is a different kind of reading. It is revelatory teaching...gained...in the Holy Presence.
– MONA JOHNIAN

By His grace He has given Pastor David Swan the master key that will bring about a revival of Davidic Worship. **– PAUL JOHNIAN**

It has helped steer me deeper in my calling as a prophetic worship minister. The truths you shared are increasingly precious and clear in these last days.
– PASTOR PAUL SOONG

PASSION FOR THE GLORY

"That you may know...the riches of the glory." (Eph 1:18)

The end–time move of the Spirit involves a restoration of the glory to the Bride of Christ. With the restoration of the glory, there will be a restoration of spiritual authority and power. The Heavenly Father and the Holy Spirit will not fail to present unto Jesus — the Bridegroom — a holy, glorious, radiant, mature, beautiful and powerful Bride. In His glory, there is an energising and empowering. In His glory, a divine exchange transpires which will enrich and transform your life.

Among the 48 topics covered are
- Pathway to the Glory
- The Spirit of Excellence
- Sons of Glory
- From Glory to Glory
- Benefits & Blessings of the Glory
- Hungering for the Glory
- Carrying the Glory
- The Garments of Glory and Beauty
- Full of Glory of Ichabod?
- Levels and Degrees of Glory
- Atmosphere of Glory
- Glory Lost and Glory Recovered
- Waves of Glory
- The Glory and Revival
- The Father of Glory
- A Glorious Church

David Swan is uniquely qualified to write Passion for The Glory. I know of few others who have been so motivated by a passion for God as David has. His time and energies have been directed toward his personal quest for the Lord and His glory, and his desire to impart this knowledge to people everywhere. His intimate knowledge of the Lord and his personal experience with the manifestations of God's glory enable him to author this book.

**– PROPHETESS
RUTH WARD HEFLIN**

SONGS AND MUSIC
that minister

Michelle Tan is the eldest daughter of Rev. David Swan. She contributed and participated in the recording of the church youth album, *Beyond*, when she was sixteen. She is uniquely gifted as a singer and psalmist. The Holy Spirit has inspired her to write all the beautiful songs and music in this new album, *Better Days*.

SONG TITLES

- Beyond
- Everything Good To Me
- Better Days
- Rain On Me
- Its You

- Born To Be Free
- Thanking God For You
- At Last
- How Awesome Are You Lord
- Right Here Right Now

AVAILABLE ON CD

Tabernacle of David

BOOK ORDER FORM

Name: _____

Address: _____

_____

Tel: _____ (H) _____ (O)

QTY	BOOK TITLE	RM	US$	TOTAL
	The Davidic Generation	20	10	
	Understanding the Spiritual Seasons of Life	20	10	
	Moving into the Holy of Holies	20	10	
	The Power of Prophetic Worship	20	10	
	Passion for the Glory	20	10	
	Postage: Add RM2 per book (within Malaysia) Add US$5 per book for air mail Add US$2 per book for sea mail	2	5 2	
	Grand Total			

Please make cheque/bank draft payable to

TAN SUAN CHEW

c/o Tabernacle of David
1 Jalan Usahawan 5, Kawasan Perindustrian Setapak,
53200 Kuala Lumpur, Malaysia.
Tel: (60)3-40227530, 40227560 Fax: (60)3-40229690
E-mail: todavid@tm.net.my

CD & CASSETTE ORDER FORM

Name: _____

Address: _____

_____

Tel: _____ (H) _____ (O)

QTY	CD TITLE	RM	US$	TOTAL
	Blessing – Mandarin Album	25	12	
	Beyond – Youth Album	25	12	
	Jamahan Roh Kudus – Malay Album	25	12	
	Music & Scriptures	30	12	
	Mighty Jehovah	30	12	
	Michelle - Better Days	30	12	
	CASSETTE TITLE			
	Prophetic Songs	10	6	
	Prophetic Songs 2	10	6	
	Blessing – Mandarin Album	10	6	
	Beyond – Youth Album	10	6	
	Jamahan Roh Kudus – Malay Album	10	6	
	Music & Scriptures	12	6	
	Mighty Jehovah	12	6	
	Michelle - Better Days	12	6	
	Postage:			
	Add RM1 per CD/tape (within Malaysia)	1		
	Add US$2 per CD/tape for air mail		2	
	Add US$1 per CD/tape for sea mail		1	
	Grand Total			

Please make cheque/bank draft payable to

TABERNACLE OF DAVID

1 Jalan Usahawan 5, Kawasan Perindustrian Setapak,
53200 Kuala Lumpur, Malaysia.
Tel: (60)3-40227530, 40227560 Fax: (60)3-40229690
E-mail: todavid@tm.net.my

Tabernacle of David

New Millennium
PROPHETIC WORSHIP SCHOOL

Principal: David Swan   Commencing: **March to May, year 2000**

Some of the subjects to be covered:

- The Sweet Psalmist of Israel - The Life of David
- The Spiritual Dynamics of Prophetic Worship
- The Realm of the Holy of Holies
- The Power of the Voice
- The Power of Prophetic Worship
- The New Millennium Church
- The Worship Reformation
- Synergising the Various Anointings
- Davidic Worship
- Spiritual Warfare
- Prophetic Music and Songs
- Perils and Pitfalls of the Music Ministry
- Music in Scriptures
- Leaders in Worship - The Leader
- An Eternal Ministry - The Ministry of Worship

Some of the courses available:

- Track Production & Studio Recording
- Timbrel & Dance (Devotion in Motion)
- The Shophar
- Sound Systems
- Prophetic Worship Leading
- Keyboard Techniques
- Flags Twirling
- Banners Making
- Vocals

Course include practical exposure in church worship services and convention.

Lecturers/Instructors: David Swan ◆ **Guest Lecturers** ◆ **TOD Ministerial Staff**

TABERNACLE OF DAVID
321A Lorong T.A.R. Kanan Satu, Off Jalan Tuanku Abdul Rahman,
50300 Kuala Lumpur, Malaysia.   Tel: (6)03-2929297 / 2912701 / 2949448
Fax: (6)03-2918301   Email: todavid@tm.net.my   Website: www.todavid-worship.org